Aphantasia

Journeying Through Mind Blindness and Celebrating Our Unique Neurodiversity with Passion and Purpose

Joanne Hedger

Elemental

Elemental Retail Ltd

Contents

Introduction

Let me start by telling you about my "moment of realization" because quite frankly that's where all this started. It hit me quite late in life, in my 40s in fact, I had been blissfully unaware up until that point, I just thought I was a bit slow at getting jokes, had a dodgy memory, and didn't dream the same way other people seemed to. Nothing unusual, we are all different and I just put these things down on my growing list of personal quirks.

It was during one of those casual group get-togethers, you know the ones where close friends catch up and share stories, we all laugh, day turns to night and we keep laughing, enjoying each other's latest life calamities and bantering till the early hours.

A friend recounted a story about a recent embarrassing event that involved a tray of red wine in glasses, a full face plant, and some mild, but accidental body exposure. As everyone erupted into laughter, I found myself nodding along, caught up in the contagious giggles of those around me. But as the punchline approached, my laughter faltered, replaced by the all-familiar sinking feeling of utter confusion. It's not *that* funny? What are they laughing at?

It's common for me when a joke relies so much on visuals – the description of the panicked look, the mortified shock on the gathered faces, and the frantic scrambling of friends to cover dignity and mop up the mess. As usual, the only thing scrambling was my brain. I was left slightly bewildered, struggling to put together the scant descriptions my friend was verbalizing and being more concerned about how that poor person must have felt, were they injured? and how on earth were they going to get red wine stains out? I just couldn't find much funny in it at all and assumed that everyone else, like me, was now laughing more at each other rather than the joke. But then someone else continued, "I can just picture it now, like a scene from a horror film..." I don't even remember how the rest of the conversation went, but after another punchline and more laughter, it finally dawned on me that they weren't speaking metaphorically at all. They could actually *picture* it. As in, see it in their mind like a high-definition movie.

I felt an unexpected pang of isolation. Like I was a spectator, standing on the outside looking in, no longer able to fully immerse myself in the shared laughter and camaraderie. As the joke reached its climax and the laughter subsided, I couldn't help but feel a twinge of sadness – not for the joke itself, but for the realization that my mind's eye was blind.

A few exposing questions and some frantic Googling soon confirmed it, and suddenly, a lifetime of blank stares at visual jokes and the utter confusion at "paint a picture in your mind" made horrifying, yet liberating, sense. I am mind blind, or to use the proper label, I am at the blind end of a mental imagery spectrum, which is known as **Aphantasia**, along with about 4% of the population (although I have no idea where they get that figure from as most people I speak to have never heard the term before, let alone know if they have it or not!).

It was a defining moment, and although it was accompanied by a massive sense of loss and longing, it also sparked a newfound curiosity and determination within me. From that day to this, I have been on a journey of self-discovery and more recently self-acceptance (although FOMO still looms large in my world as a result).

This book isn't intended to be a self-indulgent sharing of my journey; it's more a mission. A mission to shine a light on aphantasia, embracing it not as just another trendy new label, but as a unique perspective of experiencing the world. For some, it simply does not exist, it's just one end of a spectrum we are all part of, so this book aims to put forward all those views in a balanced and non-judgemental way. I'm no expert, nor am I a psychologist, but I have truly immersed myself in the "scene" and so there will be some science, some personal tales, and, yes, even some perks to being "mind blind" (who knew being spoiler-proof was a thing?).

I've been shocked, fascinated, and even disappointed at times. I've heard all kinds of viewpoints on the so-called "benefits" of being mind-blind, which for some are not benefits at all, and this very understanding has proven to me that we are all so different, so unique, despite being given the same label. Neurodiversity is a hot topic and I personally believe no two people are wired the same way, so this book is an exploration of how we, the neurodiverse mind-blind individuals (the aphants), navigate the world despite not being able to see it in our heads. It's my attempt at explaining how we still have imagination, we still share experiences and create lasting memories, just in our own ways, and of course, it's not going to be the same for everyone, some content you will agree with and some you won't, especially if you are reading this as someone with "acquired" aphantasia, and that's ok.

This book is not just for the aphants, it's also for the friends, the families, and the partners of aphants who've ever wondered what it must be like and how differently we can experience the same world. Through stories from our community, the media, and recent research studies, you'll see that aphantasia is in no way a hindrance, but rather a unique way to process information, record memories and experience life just as deeply, I believe, as those with full mental imagery might.

Beyond the science and the stories, this book is also a call to arms for empathy, advocacy, and for a world that recognizes and celebrates the kaleidoscope of human thinking. This book is your invitation to join that cause, to learn, laugh, and maybe even see the world a little differently.

Here's to discovering that sometimes, *not* seeing is believing.

Chapter 1:
The Aphantasia Experience

Let's start with the basics...

For an estimated 1-4% of the population, the canvas of the mind's eye remains blank, not due to a lack of desire or creative thought, but because of a phenomenon recently labeled as "aphantasia". It's a term that may not ring bells for everyone, but for those in the know, it's a significant part of their perception of the world and themselves.

For many, being "in the know" doesn't happen until much later in life, which is odd because the concept of the mind's eye stretches back centuries. Aphantasia is a unique wiring of the brain and simply means a different way of processing, thinking, and remembering, distinct from the visual narratives that many take for granted.

This chapter provides insights into its definition, origins, and the spectrum it covers.

1.1 Unpacking Aphantasia

Definition and Scope

The term 'aphantasia' comes from the Greek words for 'without' and 'phantasy', suggesting a lack of mental imagery. At its core, aphantasia is characterized by "**an individual's inability to voluntarily create mental images.**"

While the concept might sound straightforward, its implications reach deep, affecting how we remember past events, imagine future scenarios, and even dream.

It's important to understand that aphantasia is not a lack of imagination or creativity (so important that I may repeat this many times throughout this book!). Many individuals with aphantasia excel in creative professions, finding unique ways to express their ingenuity without relying on mental visualization.

Public Awareness

The general awareness of aphantasia has seen a significant uptick in recent years, thanks in part to social media and the increased interest of the scientific community. People from various walks of life have begun sharing their experiences, shedding light on how this condition affects their daily lives and creative processes. Such discussions have enabled a broader understanding and acceptance of aphantasia. One Aphantasia Facebook group, at the time of writing, has over 21 thousand members and is where I spent a crazy amount of time scrolling when I first found out.

This growing awareness has also prompted more researchers to study aphantasia, aiming to uncover its neurological foundations and potential impacts on learning, memory, and creativity.

It's one of the main reasons for putting this book together. When I first discovered the term, I bought all 3 books I could find on the subject – but it was simply not enough. Since then, there have been further books published along with scientific papers, research study results, and personal memoirs. Social media groups and websites have also sprung up in support of this neurodivergence. This book aims to bring together much of this information into a single introductory resource (using non-scientific jargon) for those newly aware of the condition, in the hope that the information can be shared further and wider than before.

Initial Discovery and History

The term 'aphantasia' was coined relatively recently, in 2015, by Professor Adam Zeman, a cognitive and behavioral neurologist at the University of Exeter. However, the phenomenon it describes is far from new. Historical accounts suggest that individuals have experienced and documented aspects of aphantasia for centuries, albeit without a formal name or understanding.

Zeman's work brought much-needed attention and a framework for discussing the condition, sparking interest both within the scientific community and among the general public. This pivotal moment marked the beginning of a new chapter in understanding the diversity of human cognitive experiences.

Discovering aphantasia caused me to challenge preconceived notions about how people think, learn, remember, and create. It forced me to look again at the seemingly endless ways in which the mind works and adapts. Just because we cannot visualize the chess board five moves ahead, does not mean we cannot be a grandmaster; we just plan things differently in our heads. Just because some of us struggle to recall the images that form sheet music, does not mean we can never learn to play an instrument. In fact, countless aphants have made a very good living as professional musicians, music teachers, and songwriters.

1.2 The Mind's Eye: What It Means to Be "Mind Blind"

Before discovering aphantasia, I had always thought it was just a figure of speech when people spoke about "seeing" with the mind's eye. I would often hear people respond to comments with the phrase "I see what you're saying", which I guess deaf people do when lip-reading, but most of the time what they mean is "I *hear* what you are saying". Turns out this was not the case, people do in fact *see* what others are saying... in mental images – just not me. I can only hear and then conceptualize what is being said. I remember the overwhelming shock when I realized other people were creating pictures in their heads. Some friends claim to be able to create mental images as effortlessly as flipping through a photo album, so effortlessly in fact that they could even do it with their eyes open! I was so blown away.

If I'm honest with myself, despite endlessly studying the topic, I still struggle to wrap my head around it, even today. I often wonder about the movie technique filmmakers use where they slow down footage to represent the mental imagery of a character. It's typically used when the character is infatuated with someone; for example, a guy might view a woman he fancies walking along a street, and we are shown a slowed-down version of her such that we are led to believe she is bathed in golden light, her hair flowing behind her, etc. Is this portrayal representative of what people can do in their minds? Can people really exaggerate reality like that whenever they want to? Some friends that I question can, and others not so much. Fascinating.

When I first discovered that a mind's eye was a real thing, I would spend ages sitting in a quiet room trying as hard as I could to turn my thoughts into pictures. I would try with my eyes open and then my eyes closed. I would try to think of things I knew extremely well or saw often, like the dashboard of my car, or the kitchen sink, but nothing worked. Resolutely blank. The most upsetting for me was realizing that other people could visualize faces in their minds as well. If I want to remember someone, I must go through my photo gallery. It possibly explains why I have always been such a keen photographer – constantly capturing and documenting my life in images.

The months that followed my realization were filled with questions, unsatisfactory answers, more questions, and a whole bunch of things that suddenly made sense. Like why I could never understand the concept of counting sheep to help you get to sleep... what sheep? who's sheep? where do I find them? Totally bewildered.

I joined forums, filled in questionnaires, and took part in research studies. I spent time on social media groups and read a huge number of stories and experiences from people with aphantasia, both of how they discovered it and also how they naturally work around it and adapt. The range is extremely varied. Some realize they're different when they learn that not everyone resorts to organizing their thoughts as bullet points or structured outlines. One person might describe the process of remembering as a list of facts, devoid of visual scenes, while another talks about dreaming in emotions and sounds rather than images. Some aphants don't see it as a challenge at all, while others feel huge relief at having an understanding and a known label to search with. Then there are also plenty of sad stories of people who have struggled with it for years and have not been able to cope or adapt.

Emotional and Cognitive Effects

The emotional and cognitive landscape of someone with aphantasia is just as rich and complex as those without, it just appears to be navigated differently. Without visual memories, emotions tied to past events can be less vivid, making certain therapeutic and relaxation techniques, like visualization-based meditation, quite pointless and certainly less effective. However, this doesn't mean emotions are felt less deeply. I can still cry when reading a particularly moving book, yet at the same time, there are a lot of authors I cannot get on with simply because they either include too many characters that I cannot keep track of, or they spend too long describing the visual details of every scene to the point where I lose interest.

There also seems to be a lot of misinformation floating about. I've seen aphantasia being stamped as the cause of all kinds of things that may or may not be linked (like left-handedness, poor dress sense, and even an inability to sing!), but in reality, the research simply hasn't been done yet, so these statements cannot be confirmed either way. Coincidentally, these are all things that do apply to me!

I've read claims that PTSD and emotional trauma are "less severe" for aphants simply because we don't relive the visuals, yet I have read an equal number of disputes from aphants who suffer horrific PTSD, complete with sounds, physical bodily reactions, and terrifying emotions as real as the day the trauma occurred. So, in my opinion, the emotional effects are so wide and varied that until more studies have been completed, it's impossible to say how being mind-blind might affect us. We must keep an open mind, although I must say, I am very thankful that I cannot visually relive in my mind certain events from my past. It also makes sense to me now why I never understood the phrase "well that can never be unseen".

Coping Mechanisms

I accept that not being able to see things in our minds changes how we solve problems and come up with new ideas. It's thought that people with aphantasia tend to be really good at thinking abstractly (another unproven claim, but one that does make sense). We're great at finding solutions without needing to picture them. This different way of thinking can bring fresh ideas, especially in areas where seeing things isn't the only important factor, and shows that being **different isn't deficient**.

There's no doubt about it, living in a world that's pretty much designed for the visually imaginative requires adaptation. It's such a common question on forums and group chats, that I thought I'd include some adaptation strategies that have popped up as suggestions time and time again, and proven useful for individuals with aphantasia;

- **Lists and Structured Notes**: For tasks that others might approach with mental visualization, like planning an event or organizing a space, making detailed lists and notes becomes indispensable.

- **Verbal Rehearsal**: Memorisation and recall can pose challenges without mental images to anchor information. Instead, verbal rehearsal—repeating information aloud or in your head—tends to work well for embedding knowledge in the shorter term.

- **Training Other Senses**: Focusing on the non-visual senses—touch, taste, smell, and hearing—enriches experiences and

memories. For example, associating a specific scent with a loved
one or a piece of music with a significant event creates powerful
non-visual anchors for memory.

- **Embracing Technology**: In the digital age, technology offers
  numerous ways to organize and "brain-dump" our thoughts.
  We will look in more detail at these tools in chapter 4.

- **Peer Support and Sharing Strategies**: Connecting with others who experience the world similarly can be incredibly validating. I certainly felt less like a freak among my friends when
  I joined groups and started sharing questions and experiences
  with others who think the same way.

Each of these strategies proves the fundamental truth about aphantasia: it's a variation in human experience, not a limitation. The ability to
think, create, remember, and dream takes many forms. For those of us
with aphantasia, the journey involves discovering and honing the tools
that work best for us, crafting an experience of the world that's rich in
detail, sensation, and understanding, even if it's not seen in the mind's
eye.

We will look in more detail at each of these coping strategies in later
chapters.

1.3 A Spectrum of Imagination

As we've touched on already, one of the most fascinating aspects of
aphantasia is its variability. Just as no two fingerprints are the same, the
experience of aphantasia differs from one individual to the next. Some
report a complete absence of mental imagery across all senses (sight,

sound, taste, touch, scent), while others (like me) find only visual imagery to be elusive. This variability also extends to memory and dreaming.

Recognizing this spectrum is crucial for avoiding one-size-fits-all assumptions about how it affects those who experience it. At one end is **Aphantasia**, where individuals have little to no ability to visualize mental images, and at the other end is **Hyperphantasia**, where individuals experience extremely vivid and detailed mental imagery.

Here's an outline of the basic categories;

- **Aphantasia**: Difficulty or inability to generate images in your mind's eye. Relying on other senses or conceptual thinking rather than visualizing.

- **Hypophantasia / Low Visualization**: Some ability to visualize but with limited clarity, detail, or consistency. Mental images may be faint, fleeting, or difficult to maintain. They might struggle to picture scenes or objects vividly.

- **Average Visualization**: Most people fall into this category, where they possess a moderate ability to visualize mental images. They can conjure up images with a reasonable amount of detail and clarity, though not as vividly as those with hyperphantasia.

- **Phantasia / High Visualization**: Individuals with high visualization skills can generate mental images with greater clarity, detail, and consistency compared to the average person. They may find it easier to immerse themselves in their imaginations and visualize scenes or objects vividly.

- **Hyperphantasia**: An extreme end of the spectrum where individuals experience exceptionally vivid and detailed mental imagery. They can create images in their mind's eye with extraordinary clarity, almost as if they were seeing them in the physical world. This level of visualization may be accompanied by intense sensory experiences and strong emotional responses.

It's important to note that the spectrum is not limited to these categories and can vary widely among individuals. Factors such as genetics, brain structure, and personal experiences can influence where someone falls on this spectrum. Additionally, visualization abilities may change over time due to practice, training, or neurological changes.

Believe it or not, I am still a little undecided about where I sit on the scale, I can hear, smell, taste, and touch in my head, but I don't see any images at all. However I know I have dreamt in pictures on occasion, so perhaps it's only my conscious mind that is blind, but my subconscious is not!? Again, this is something we will explore as we move through this book.

1.4 Discovering Aphantasia

Recognizing that you have aphantasia often happens by accident and is typically marked by moments of confusion, revelation, and in my case, huge FOMO. Some are lucky enough to come across it online as an intro video or social media post related to something else, or more recently a newspaper article in the mainstream media. But for many, it's a mind-blowing realization triggered by a question of a friend or relative. The question is typically asked because we have suspicions that our brains work differently, or because we simply cannot grasp something that's happening in the same way other people appear to.

Early Signs

These early signs or suspicions are subtle, often mistaken for quirks or simply different ways of thinking. I've listed some common experiences here, but again this list is not exhaustive, and remember it is also not the same for everyone;

- Difficulty in following instructions that require visual imagination, like the classic that is usually given during a relaxation exercise or yoga class to "picture yourself on a beach". Instead of blue sky and white sand, the mind's screen stays stubbornly blank, causing aphants to question why they bother doing this exercise when there's nothing to see.

- Challenges in recalling visual details of past events. While others recount the color of guests' outfits worn at a wedding, or the look of a favorite restaurant from a trip years ago, individuals with aphantasia might only remember they were pleasant experiences, devoid of any visual snapshot.

- A preference for lists and written directions over maps or spatial instructions. Navigating new places becomes a logical activity rather than a visual journey.

- The ability to rewatch TV programs almost as if you had never seen them before.

- Difficulty reading fictional novels, particularly those with more than a handful of characters. In my experience, these books typically have a heavy focus on describing each character visually at the start which, because it is pointless for me, can get tedious to read after a while. I then spend the remainder of the book flicking back to the start to remind myself who each character is each time they crop up. It is tricky to hold the storyline like this.

• When a book is made into a movie someone without a mind's eye will never comment on the casting to say... "oh that's not how I pictured him" – We don't picture anything at all when reading a book!

• Inability to find visual jokes funny; Especially those told by stand-up comedians, like Eddie Murphy, whose whacky stories are designed to invite the audience to picture exaggerated, outrageous scenarios. There is also an uncomfortable delay for me with jokes that require me to work out the punchline myself – typically because these jokes rely on the audience creating a mental picture... for example; my partner recently responded to the question *what do you fancy for dinner?* with "Pork Wellington" – which took me way too long to realize he meant sausage rolls. I'm guessing that had I have been able to picture a pork Wellington instantly in my mind, I would have laughed at his attempt to hide the fact that he wanted junk food for dinner. Instead, I replied, "Oh I didn't know we had any pork", he just looked at me amused. I went on, "In fact, I don't think I know how to make pork wellington", he continued to look at me blankly, waiting for the penny to drop. Eventually, I cottoned on and groaned in realization, but of course, the gag was wasted on me and I was left feeling just a little bit dim!

These early indicators, though seemingly inconsequential at the time, lay the groundwork for a later realization that our minds operate differently from others, such that when you discover aphantasia, all these little things put together suddenly make perfect sense. The pieces fall into place, and the experiences that once felt isolating now have a name.

For me I remember feeling so relieved at having an explanation for my appalling memory, my total disinterest in visual meditation, and my inability to find many jokes funny. But most of all, I could finally get my head around what Johnnie Wilkinson was doing each time he prepared himself to kick the ball between those rugby posts!

A common "moment of revelation" seems to come from discussions about daydreaming. While many revel in their ability to lose themselves in vivid mental narratives, those with aphantasia find the concept bewildering. The realization that "daydreaming" implies actual visual dreaming during the day can be a watershed moment.

I always assumed daydreaming was simply staring blankly out at the view because your mind was occupied thinking about other things, I had never appreciated the fact that people were genuinely creating movies in their minds, or "seeing" their dreams played out in images in their heads. Mad!

Of course, when you realize it, you immediately want to find out who else is in the same boat as you, so you ask everyone closest to you. I have bored my friends to tears with questions on the topic and tests for them – trying to understand exactly what they are seeing in their minds and how they do it. The answers are also varied, some can augment reality as and when they choose; animating artwork or imagining how something might look if moved from one side of the room to another, others can pull up pictures on request as if from a library, while most get pictures of objects or people delivered automatically to their mind at the mere mention of them – something I might consider intrusive and potentially annoying, unless it was images from my bird book of course – then it would be pretty damn handy!

Impact on Self-Perception

Realizing you have aphantasia and accepting it can change how you see yourself, affecting how you think and create things in your mind. If you are anything like me, this discovery initially makes you feel like you're missing out on something everyone else experiences and clearly brings them a lot of joy and entertainment.

As I said, this feeling of missing out was particularly hard for me when I realized that other people could recall the faces of lost friends and family members whenever they felt like it. Of course, I know how to describe people from information stored in my brain; my Mum, for example, has blonde hair, in a bob, with a short fringe, and is slightly taller than me, but I cannot bring an image of her to my mind at all. I need to look at a photo for that. I have always been absolutely blown away by anyone who can create one of those identikit images they use to help solve crimes, I guess I assumed it was just for TV and that people couldn't really do that unless they had a photographic memory. Turns out 96% of the population probably can and just 4% of us cannot!

However, this fear of missing out eventually gives way to a deeper self-acceptance and a re-evaluation of personal strengths. The inability to visualize becomes less about what's lacking and more about the unique ways in which the mind operates. Turns out I experience things in my mind that others don't simply because they have no need to... because they can picture things instead. Let me explain. A while back I was on a canal boat trip with friends and we visited the beautiful village of Foxton in middle England, where the impressive **Foxton Incline**

Plane was built over 100 years ago, as a shortcut to taking your boat down the two 5-lock staircases which would have taken over three hours. There is a museum there that describes exactly how the Incline Plane would have operated and explains that thousands of people would have turned out to witness the first boats being carried in huge containers up the hillside. As we left the museum and climbed up to stand on the viewing platform overlooking the hillside, my mind started to recreate the atmosphere of that opening day in the early 1900's. I might not have been able to see the scene in front of me, but I could hear market sellers calling to advertise their wares to the visitors, I could smell the horses that would have been waiting to carry on tugging boats down the towpath, and I could feel the squelch of churned mud beneath my boots made by the thousands of people in the crowd. When I chatted with my friends more recently about our experiences at that viewing platform it seemed as if theirs were much simpler than mine. They were of course able to picture the boats going up and down and marvelled at the engineering of it all, but I can't help thinking that my experience felt richer somehow, well to think of it like that certainly reduced my FOMO a bit anyway!

For me, this shift in self-perception gave me a newfound appreciation for the brain's adaptability and the diverse ways it can interpret the world. Especially when curious friends would ask questions about how I performed certain tasks without being able to see them, it forced me to think about how I actually do it. This in turn strengthens the idea that there's no single right way to think, remember, or imagine.

Chapter 2: Perceptions and Misconceptions

2.1 Beyond the Myths

You're at a party, and the topic of imagination comes up. Someone mentions they can't visualize anything in their mind's eye, and the room splits. Half are fascinated, asking a million questions, while the rest are convinced it's a desperate play for attention. If it sounds familiar, it's because it is a common scenario for anyone with aphantasia trying to explain their experience. This chapter aims to clear the air, offering clarity and debunking some of the myths about aphantasia. So, let's set the record straight, shall we?

Defining Clearly

I'll say it again.... Aphantasia, in its simplest form, means the absence of a mind's eye – the inability to voluntarily create mental images. **It's not about lacking imagination or creativity**; it's about how our brain processes and recalls visual information. A person with aphantasia can be just as creative, intelligent, and successful as anyone else; they just experience their thoughts differently.

Common Myths

- **Myth #1: "People with aphantasia can't imagine or be creative."** Not true. Creativity isn't only visual. Many individuals with aphantasia excel in creative fields, leveraging their other senses, conceptual thinking, or their knack for problem-solving in unique ways.

- **Myth #2: "Aphantasia is a disability."** Again, not accurate. While it indeed presents challenges, especially in a world designed for the visually minded, those born with aphantasia naturally adapt and often develop enhanced abilities in other areas, such as logic and focus. To the point where most live their entire lives without realizing that there is anything different about their "wiring", and even after discovery, agree that it hasn't hindered them in any way. It's just a quirk of brain function.

- **Myth #3: "Everyone with aphantasia experiences it the same way."** This is a misunderstanding. Just like any aspect of human cognition, there's a spectrum. Some might have a partial ability to visualize, while others might not visualize at all but can engage other senses vividly in their mind.

- **Myth #4: Aphants don't know what they're missing so why does it matter?** Not everyone with aphantasia was born with it, some people have been known to "acquire" it later in life after some significant event, trauma, psychological disturbance, etc. So they really do notice the difference, they know exactly what they're missing, and also have not developed any kind of coping mechanisms or memory adaptations, so find it extremely difficult to adjust.

Expert Opinions

Neuroscientists and psychologists have weighed in, offering insights that help demystify aphantasia. Research suggests that aphantasia simply involves a different neurological pathway for accessing and processing sensory information. This variation in brain function is part of the broader spectrum of human neurodiversity, highlighting the incredible range of how people perceive and interact with the world around them.

Personal Testimonies

Real-life experiences often speak louder than theories. Consider Sarah, a graphic designer who can't visualize images but has developed a keen sense of spatial awareness and a deep understanding of colour theory and design principles. Or take Alex, a writer who crafts detailed narratives without picturing scenes in their mind, focusing on dialogue, emotion, and the flow of ideas to tell a story. These testimonies shatter the stereotype that aphantasia limits one's ability to create, innovate, or succeed.

In discussions about aphantasia, clarity matters. By defining what aphantasia is (and isn't), tackling myths head-on, considering expert insights, and listening to those who live with it every day, we can generate a more accurate and empathetic understanding of this fascinating condition. Whether at that party, in a classroom, or going about your daily business, having the facts at your fingertips makes all the difference.

2.2 The Stigma of Being Different

Living your life with aphantasia is not just about the internal experience of missing mental imagery or the FOMO that comes with it; it's also about facing the external world's misconceptions and ignorance. For some, these biases can cast long shadows, affecting how individuals with aphantasia see themselves and interact with the world.

I personally chatted it through with my closest friends and family but then stopped telling people after the initial realization wore off, not because I don't see it as a disability (I don't), but because I found it so difficult to explain. No one else sees the world how I see it or processes memories how I do. We are all unique.

Societal Biases

In a society that celebrates vivid imagination and visual creativity, we would expect to find aphantasia on the outskirts of accepted norms. The inability to visualize mistakenly being equated with a lack of creativity or intelligence, leading to unfair judgments and/or social isolation. But thankfully due to the relatively recent adoption of the term, and therefore the widespread lack of awareness about the condition, these social biases have not yet developed into particularly large issues, well not for me anyway. In my experience, people tend to be more curious than judgemental, and many simply do not believe the condition warrants being labeled. This could be for a number of reasons; just as it's difficult to explain, it's also difficult for those with visual cognition to grasp the concept that our mind's eye can be blind.

That said, misconceptions could easily lead to individuals being overlooked for creative projects or roles, under the false assumption that they lack imaginative capabilities, so it is something you may want to consider carefully before sharing with your work colleagues or potential employers.

Role of Education

Education plays a pivotal role in reducing the risk of prejudice. It's not just about informing the public about what aphantasia is; it's about reshaping the narrative around imagination, creativity, and intelligence.

- **Incorporating Neurodiversity in Curriculum**: Including information about neurodiversity and conditions like aphantasia in educational materials can encourage early understanding and acceptance.

- **Professional Development for Educators**: Training teachers and educational professionals to recognize and support diverse cognitive experiences can create more inclusive learning environments. It would certainly have helped me if there had been alternative methods of teaching – particularly for visual lessons like history or geometry!

- **Public Awareness Campaigns**: Initiatives aimed at the general public, explaining the spectrum of human experience, can reduce stigma and build a culture of acceptance and curiosity rather than judgment.

2.3 Aphantasia in Popular Culture

When you flick through channels, scroll down your streaming service, or lose yourself in the pages of a novel, how often do you encounter a character who navigates the world with aphantasia? The answer, for now, might be closer to seldom, if ever. Let's take a brief moment to think about how aphantasia is making its way into movies, TV shows, and literature, the impact of these portrayals, and how a shift towards more accurate representation could help raise awareness.

Current Representation

In the realm of pop culture, aphantasia remains a largely unknown concept, often overshadowed by more visually dramatic narratives. However, a few pioneering works have begun to include this unique way of experiencing the world in their stories. For instance, a novel might feature a protagonist who, unable to visualize their lost love's face, focuses instead on the texture of their hand or the sound of their laugh. A TV drama might showcase a detective who, devoid of the ability to picture crime scenes mentally, relies on meticulous notetaking and a keen sense of detail to solve cases.

These instances, while few and far between, open a window for audiences to glimpse the inner workings of a mind without mental imagery. They hint at the depth and richness of experiencing life differently, challenging the notion that visual imagination is the sole gateway to creativity and emotional depth.

The Power of Accurate Representation

As with all kinds of neurodiversity, the significance of getting it right cannot be overstated. When media portrayals of aphantasia are nuanced and informed, they do more than entertain; they educate. Accurate representation can dismantle myths, encourage empathy, and offer validation to those who see their experiences reflected on screen or in print.

For viewers or readers unfamiliar with aphantasia, these portrayals can be eye-opening, illuminating the challenges and triumphs of living a life with different mental wiring. For individuals with aphantasia, seeing our experiences mirrored in pop culture would be profoundly validating. A signal that our way of processing the world is recognized, valued, and worthy of exploration in stories that reach wide audiences.

Advocating for Better Representation

While the growing presence of aphantasia in pop culture is promising, there's ample room for growth. Here's how we can push for a broader, more accurate representation:

- **Support Pioneering Works**: When movies, shows, or books get it right, support them. Watch, read, share, and talk about these works. High engagement not only rewards efforts to diversify storytelling but also signals to the industry that audiences are interested in and value these narratives.

- **Create and Share**: If you're inclined, create your own stories, scripts, or artworks that reflect the aphantasic experience. Platforms like blogs, social media, and independent publishing offer spaces to share these creations in an easy, free, and often enjoyable way.

- **Feedback and Dialogue**: Reach out to creators, writers, and producers. Social media and digital platforms offer direct lines of communication to share insights, express the need for diverse representation, and offer perspectives on portraying aphantasia with accuracy and depth.

Chapter 3: Peering into the Science of Aphantasia

The quest to understand aphantasia takes us deep into the inner workings of the human brain. This section aims to shed light on how our brains process, or in some cases don't process, visual information in the traditional sense.

Imagine trying to study a shadow by the light it doesn't cast. The science of aphantasia feels a bit like that because it's about understanding a phenomenon largely by what's missing or different rather than what's overtly present.

So, let's sift through the current scientific landscape surrounding aphantasia, the studies, the head-scratchers, and the eureka moments that define this field.

3.1 The Current State of Research: What We Know So Far

Overview of Studies

Research on aphantasia, while still in its infancy, has started to sketch the outlines of this intriguing condition. Early studies, primarily led by cognitive neurologist Adam Zeman, laid the groundwork by identifying and naming aphantasia, bringing it into the scientific and public discourse. Following Zeman's lead, a smattering of studies have begun to explore the prevalence of aphantasia, its impact on memory and imagination, and the brain's wiring in those who experience it.

One key study involved participants attempting to visualize a series of objects. Those with aphantasia showed markedly less activity in the brain's regions associated with visual processing compared to their imagining counterparts. This stark contrast provided concrete evidence that aphantasia isn't just a quirk of personality or a lack of effort but a distinct way the brain functions.

Visualization Pathways

To grasp how aphantasia might arise, it's crucial to understand the normal pathways involved in visualization. The brain's ability to conjure images relies on a network of regions, including the frontal cortex, which handles higher cognitive functions, and the visual cortex, where sensory information from the eyes is processed. When we visualize, these areas work in tandem, with the frontal cortex generating the 'request' for an image and the visual cortex producing the 'picture.'

In aphantasia, this collaboration appears to falter. The signal from the frontal cortex may be sent, but the visual cortex doesn't respond in the usual way, leading to an absence of mental imagery. This disruption could stem from differences in connectivity or activity levels within this network, though the exact mechanisms are still under investigation.

Neurological Differences

Recent studies have begun to pinpoint specific neural differences in individuals with aphantasia compared to those who can visualize "normally". For instance, research indicates variations in the connectivity and functionality of the brain's network responsible for visual processing and memory. One notable study used functional magnetic resonance imaging (fMRI) to observe the brains of people with and without aphantasia as they performed tasks requiring visual imagination. Results showed distinct patterns of brain activity between the two groups, particularly in areas known to be involved in generating visual images. Those with aphantasia exhibited less activity in the visual cortex when trying to visualize.

The Role of Memory

The interplay between memory and visualization is intricate, with visual memories serving as the building blocks for mental images. For those with aphantasia, recalling visual details of past events can be challenging, raising questions about how the brain compensates for this gap in visual recollection.

Research suggests that individuals with aphantasia might rely more heavily on non-visual forms of memory, such as factual or semantic memory. Instead of "seeing" a past event, they might recall details about it—facts, figures, and descriptions—without the accompanying imagery. This reliance on alternative memory systems demonstrates the brain's remarkable ability to adapt and find new pathways for processing information.

When we examine dreaming in individuals with aphantasia, it sheds further light on memory function. Despite our inability to visualize during waking hours, some aphants report having vivid dreams. This suggests that the brain's ability to create visual imagery may still be present in some capacity, perhaps activated during different states of consciousness or utilizing alternative pathways compared to conscious visualization.

Methodological Challenges

Studying aphantasia comes with its set of hurdles. The biggest one? The subjectivity of mental experiences. How do you measure the absence of an image in the mind's eye or compare the vividness of mental imagery across individuals? Researchers have leaned on questionnaires and brain imaging techniques like fMRI to bridge this gap, but the subjective nature of visualization still makes quantifying and understanding aphantasia a tough nut to crack. How do we prove that what I "think" in my mind isn't the same as what non-aphants are "seeing"?

Emerging Theories

Why does aphantasia occur, and how does it shape cognition and perception? Theories are both plentiful and fascinating. Some researchers suggest that aphantasia might stem from differences in the brain's connectivity, others propose that it could be related to the brain's memory systems, with aphantasia affecting the way visual memories are stored and retrieved.

One emerging theory suggests that aphantasia isn't just about the absence of visual imagery but could also impact how other senses and types of memories are experienced. This broadens the conversation from a purely visual phenomenon to a more holistic understanding of sensory and cognitive experiences.

Knowledge Gaps

For all the strides made, the landscape of aphantasia research is still dotted with more questions than answers. How does aphantasia affect emotions and personal relationships? Can it change over time, or is it a stable trait from birth? What are the implications for learning and creativity? And perhaps most intriguingly, can interventions or training alter the experience of those with aphantasia?

The road ahead is exciting, with each study shedding a bit more light on the enigma that is aphantasia. It's clear that this journey into the science of the mind's eye (or lack thereof) is just beginning. With every study, interview, and questionnaire, we inch closer to understanding.

3.2 Genetics vs. Environment: The Origins of Aphantasia

The question of whether aphantasia stems from our DNA or the environment we grow up in brings up the classic nature versus nurture debate. It's a puzzle that has scientists, and those of us living with aphantasia, scratching our heads. Is there a hidden code in our genes predisposing us to aphantasia, or does the condition emerge from our experiences?

Nature vs. Nurture Debate

On one hand, evidence hints at a genetic foundation for aphantasia. Studies exploring the brain's structure and function in people with aphantasia suggest innate differences that could be woven into our DNA. Yet, on the other hand, anecdotal evidence points to environmental factors, such as trauma or illness, as potential triggers for the condition.

I've spent a good deal of time pondering this myself. Did I acquire aphantasia or was I born with this wiring? Do I ever remember a time when I could mentally visualize?

Familial Patterns

Scientists focussing on family histories have noticed patterns that suggest a genetic thread might be at play. It's not uncommon for individuals with aphantasia to report relatives who also experience the world the same way, I've recently discovered that my niece also struggles to form pictures at will in her mind. This familial trend suggests that aphantasia could indeed be passed down through generations. However, without extensive genetic studies specifically targeting aphantasia, this linkage remains an educated guess rather than a scientific certainty.

Trigger Events or "Acquired Aphantasia"

Acquired aphantasia is rare, but it can occur. It's believed that something specific triggers it because it doesn't happen without a cause. For some, aphantasia appears to have emerged following a head injury, severe emotional trauma, or significant stress, suggesting that environmental factors can indeed play a pivotal role.

These personal accounts fuel the debate, highlighting the potential for the brain to adapt or change in response to experiences. They suggest a scenario where aphantasia could be the brain's response to protect itself or adapt to new circumstances.

At the time of writing only one study on acquired aphantasia has been undertaken. It found that about two-thirds of cases were related to neurological issues, like brain damage, while one-third were related to psychological factors.

This leads me to wonder whether or not I gave myself this condition in some way. Did my diving headlong into a solid cast iron radiator at about 10 years old cause this? Or was it my experimentation with mind-bending recreational drugs in the early 90's? My memory is so poor, possibly because of these things, that I simply cannot say whether I have always thought conceptually or whether I once had a perfectly functioning mind's eye. Either way, I really don't feel that it has hindered me in any way – but it does explain a lot!

There are a great many neurodiverse conditions that really do hinder people in their daily lives, but personally, I see it more as a quirk than an obstacle. That said, I have come across equal numbers of aphants who struggle with it on a daily basis for one reason or another. My heart goes out to them and I hope one-day science will help – even if only in providing more concrete answers.

So, where does the scientific community stand on the origins of aphantasia? The truth is, it's a bit of a balancing act. The prevailing view leans towards multiple origins, where both nature *and* nurture play critical roles.

3.3 Aphantasia and Memory: Understanding the Connections

Visual Memory

Visual memory plays a pivotal role in our everyday lives, more than we often realize. It's the canvas on which our past is painted, allowing us to retrieve and relive events at a moment's notice. Think of it as the mind's personal gallery, where each memory is an artwork, vivid in detail and rich in emotion. This gallery doesn't just store static images; it's dynamic, enabling us to reconstruct past events, imagine future scenarios, and even navigate the spatial complexities of our world. From recognizing faces to following a route home.

For aphants, the gallery of visual memory operates differently. The absence of mental imagery means that the artworks in this gallery are not visual but conceptual. Memories are stored and recalled not as pictures or scenes but as a collection of facts, narratives, and feelings. This distinction leads to a unique way of experiencing memories. Rather than reliving a moment in visual detail, individuals with aphantasia might recall the sequence of events, factual information, or the emotions felt at the time. This difference profoundly affects not just personal recollections but also how knowledge and experiences are internalized and retrieved.

Compensatory Mechanisms

To navigate a world where memory cannot rely on visual recall, those of us with aphantasia seem to automatically develop a variety of strategies to compensate. Here are some common ones I have come across;

- **External Aids**: Using tools and devices to externalize memory. From detailed journaling to organized collections of photographs, individuals with aphantasia often rely on external aids to capture and recall experiences. These aids serve as tangible placeholders for memories, providing a reference point that can trigger recall through non-visual means.

- **Sensory Recall**: Focusing on non-visual senses to trigger memory. For some, memories might be anchored in smells, sounds, or tactile sensations. I know a lot of people (non-aphants included) who can be instantly transported back to a specific event or location simply by getting a whiff of a particular scent or hearing a particular song or sound. Hearing gulls calling always takes me to the seaside for example, or the scent of lilac blossom takes me to my childhood bathroom where a lilac tree stood outside the window.

- **Narrative Memory**: Transforming visual scenes into detailed narratives or stories. By encoding memories as narratives, individuals with aphantasia create a structured, verbal pathway to recall information, bypassing the need for visual imagery. I will always note directions based on a list of landmarks along the way, or the sequence of turns, left, left, right for example.

- **Semantic Webs**: Leveraging connections between facts and concepts. This strategy involves creating a web of interconnected information, where one fact triggers the recall of another, building a rich web of knowledge that can be accessed without visual cues.

3.4 How Aphantasia Affects Learning

The traditional educational landscape, with its reliance on visual aids, diagrams, and the encouragement to "picture this," can present obstacles for us. Visual learning strategies, such as imagining historical events or visualizing scientific processes, might not resonate, leaving gaps in engagement and comprehension. Moreover, instructions that call for visual imagination can lead to confusion or feelings of exclusion among students with aphantasia, who might wonder why their minds don't follow the same visual paths as their peers.

The only time I can really remember it being a problem for me academically was during maths lessons, specifically geometry. I was useless at tessellating shapes and those multiple choice questions that showed a number of misshapen blocks and asked you to rotate it by 90 degrees in your head and choose the matching resultant image. Yeah, no chance. I never spent any time on those questions, just randomly picked an answer and moved on, simply because I knew however hard I stared at it, I couldn't work out *how* to work it out!

Tackling these challenges requires awareness and adaptability—both from learners and educators. Recognizing that not all students benefit from the same instructional methods is the first step toward creating an inclusive learning environment not just for aphants but for everyone. We are not alone in being different.

Learning Styles

The concept of "learning styles" has been around for a long time and proves that we don't all fit into the same mold when acquiring new knowledge. Visual, auditory, reading/writing, and kinaesthetic are the main methods covered today. Aphantasia asks us to look again at these traditional methods. For aphants, auditory and kinaesthetic learning styles might naturally take the front seat. These methods provide concrete, non-visual ways to engage with material, from listening to lectures and discussions to hands-on activities and real-world applications. For many aphants this is sufficient and making any further allowances is just not needed, but this is not the case for all. There is a fine line between alienating someone due to a perceived inability and simply providing alternative methods for someone who learns differently.

Adapting Teaching Methods

In educational settings, recognizing and catering to the diverse needs of all learners can significantly enhance their academic potential. This begins with acknowledging that the standard one-size-fits-all approach to teaching might not be the most effective route for everyone – it certainly isn't for many aphants. We know where we want to get to in the educational sense, but the traditional tools don't always work for us. It's also not necessarily about just finding a workaround, but rather discovering a whole new way to explore and absorb the knowledge that's available to us.

Here are some good practices for teachers and parents that could transform learning into an enriching experience;

- **Provide Adequate Time for Tasks**: Going back over passages of text before answering related questions is time-consuming. I found this particularly tricky during English literature when being asked to read a passage of text and then answer questions about the characters. Without having "painted a picture" of them in my mind, I would be flipping back and forth to the original text numerous times to answer each question. I was always amazed that my friends never struggled with these kinds of questions and came out of each exam declaring how easy it was or that they had loads of time at the end to enhance their answers. Now at least I know why!

- **Incorporate a Variety of Learning Materials**: Use a mix of text, audio recordings, and interactive activities to cater to different learning preferences. This approach ensures that students have multiple avenues to engage with and understand the material.

- **Create a Dialogue Around Learning Preferences**: Encourage students to share their preferred learning methods and adapt teaching strategies accordingly.

- **Verbal and Written Instructions**: For aphants, detailed verbal explanations and written instructions will be more beneficial and effective tools, and ensure we're not left trying to fill in the blanks where others see images. E.g. Asking a room full of kids to just "draw a beach scene" will generate a wide variety of pictures, but for the kid with aphantasia it will be a tricky exercise and without additional detailed instructions of what to include in the image and where to put them, you may find they simply copy the kid next to them.

- **Interactive Learning Environments**: Hands-on activities, experiments, and discussion-based classes can provide dynamic learning experiences that don't rely on visual imagery but instead engage other senses and cognitive skills.

- **Personalized Learning Plans**: Educators can work with students to develop individualized learning plans that play to their strengths, whether that's their auditory memory, analytical thinking, or creative problem-solving skills.

What can we do as students to make learning easier?

Aside from explaining to your mentor, the following approaches can make retaining information much easier;

- **Auditory Learning**: Turning to podcasts, audiobooks, and even recording your own summaries of material can tap into the auditory strengths many of us have developed. Listening to information often makes it stick better than reading the same content would.

- **Kinaesthetic Learning**: Engaging in physical activity while learning—think walking while listening to an audiobook or using fidget tools during study sessions—can help in retaining information. The movement enhances focus for many, making the learning process more active and engaging.

- **Concept Mapping**: Using tools to create flowcharts or diagrams that map out concepts and their connections can offer a visual (though not visualized) structure to information, making complex ideas easier to grasp and remember.

- **Mnemonics**: Employing mnemonic devices that use patterns of letters, ideas, or associations can aid in memorizing facts and figures. Rhymes, acronyms, and even songs can make information more memorable without needing to visualize it.

Resources for Educators and Students

Equipping both educators and students with the right tools and resources is crucial in creating an inclusive learning environment. Here's a curated list of resources that are specifically designed to support the neurodiverse (not exclusively for aphants):

- **Learning Ally**[1] : An invaluable resource offering audiobooks and text-to-speech support, making reading accessible and enjoyable for all learners.

- **Khan Academy**[2] : With its wide range of video tutorials and interactive exercises, Khan Academy caters to different learning preferences, providing an alternative to traditional textbook-based learning.

- **MindMeister**[3] : This mind mapping tool allows students and educators to organize thoughts and concepts visually, without relying on mental imagery, facilitating a better understanding of complex topics.

- **TED-Ed**[4] : A platform offering animated educational videos on a variety of subjects, making learning engaging and accessible for students who find traditional lectures challenging.

---

1. https://read.learningally.org/

2. https://www.khanacademy.org/

3. https://www.mindmeister.com/

4. https://ed.ted.com/

Lifelong Learning

The journey of learning doesn't end with formal education; it's a lifelong endeavor, and the internet has opened up huge opportunities to explore new interests, refine skills, and adapt to changing environments. Adults with aphantasia still want to learn, but we need to develop strategies that align with our preferred learning style. For me, this usually means seeking out podcasts, audiobooks, or interactive workshops on topics I am interested in because I realize these are much more successful methods for me to retain information. We don't have a TV at home, but the radio in the kitchen is nearly always on during the day and I find myself learning more through listening to interviews or podcasts than I do when I actually sit down to read and study a topic in the traditional sense. Maybe this is just my personality, but the more aphants I "meet" online, the more similarities I discover about the ways in which we like to learn.

Learning in the workplace or "professional development" can also be tailored to include aphantasia-friendly approaches, from mentorship programs that offer hands-on learning opportunities to training sessions that prioritize discussion and collaboration over visual presentations.

If you struggle with learning, but absolutely love exploring new subjects, here are some tips that will help maximize your learning potential and ensure you retain as much new knowledge as possible:

- **Follow Your Curiosity**: Let your interests lead the way. You're more likely to retain information and enjoy the learning process when you're genuinely curious about the subject. As a keen naturalist, I will never stop learning about wildlife and our green planet, and there always seems to be new research or discoveries to pique my interest.

- **Set Realistic Goals**: Break down your learning objectives into manageable steps. Celebrate your progress along the way to stay motivated. Learning apps are excellent for this, some even provide useful rewards for multi-day learning streaks which keep you moving in the right direction.

- **Join Learning Communities**: Engage with online forums, local clubs, or study groups focused on your areas of interest. These communities can offer support, resources, and the camaraderie of shared learning experiences.

- **Reflect on Your Learning**: Regularly take time to reflect on what you've learned and how you've applied it. This not only consolidates your knowledge but can also highlight areas for further exploration. I do this by regularly flicking through the notes I have made during lessons or sometimes even transferring them to a bigger scrapbook – the act of writing them out neatly, with photos or illustrations, seems to cement them in my mind far better than just putting the original notes in a folder.

It's not about compensating for what we don't have but about embracing and maximizing the incredible abilities we do have. With the right strategies, resources, and mindset, the journey of learning becomes profoundly rewarding – I would even go as far as using the word enlightening. As I've said before, I don't see mindblindness as a hindrance to learning at all, we aphants just do it in a different way – with lots of scrapbooks, notes, photographs, and voice memos (and a spreadsheet or two!).

3.5 Bridging the Gap: The Role of Other Senses in Aphantasia

In a world where one sense takes a backseat, others often step up to the plate, eager to fill the void. We know this to be true for general loss of eyesight. Blind people are usually incredibly good at picking up sounds and scents that sighted people often miss. But can the same be said for mind-blindness?

Sensory Compensation

There's growing evidence to suggest that individuals with aphantasia can indeed develop heightened abilities in their other sensory domains to provide anchors for recording memories in the absence of visual images. For example, a more acute sense of hearing that picks up nuances in music and language others might miss, or an enhanced sense of touch that can discern subtle differences in textures. These enhanced abilities can evolve into remarkable skills and talents.

I'm not convinced I have any such superpowers myself, not as a direct result of aphantasia, however, I do have a pretty good ear for bird calls and a pretty good method for making them stick in my memory. Part of my training in Africa as a safari guide included the ability to identify over 200 bird species by sound alone. I was one of fourteen students on the course, and although I struggled the most with the *visual* identification of birds, mine was the tent everyone came to at lunchtime to learn bird calls. I would play a recording of the bird call to the group, create suitable lyrics to each call to help with identification, and then by repetition we would learn half a dozen new birds every day. A wood pigeon in the UK for example sings, "I can't stop singing, I can't stop singing, I can't". I also don't find it too tricky to identify a bird by its voice rather than just relying on its call. Particularly useful when many African birds are mimics and have many different calls, but their voices remain the same.

The issue I have as an aphant is that when I hear a bird, I cannot bring to mind an image of it, even though I know what species it is. So there is often a delay for me whilst I mentally run through the information I have recorded about the bird, such as size, colour, patterning, bill shape, and inflight silhouette for example, before I know what I'm looking for in my binoculars, if we can't find the bird in the bushes, more often than not I have to get the bird book/app out and look up the bird in order to describe it to my guests. I have a UK bird ID quiz app on my phone which I am pretty good at ... because as soon as I see the bird, there is recognition and I can tell you what it is, I just can't bring up the image at will when I need it.

Personal Adaptation Strategies

The lived experiences of those with aphantasia provide us with several adaptation strategies. Here are a few notable examples that most people use, including the neurotypical, but that aphants seem to find especially helpful with regard to memory recall:

- **Soundscapes**: Creating playlists or soundscapes that encapsulate the essence of a place, event, or period in life. These serve as powerful triggers for memories and emotions, transporting the listener and helping them to reminisce despite not being able to "see" the event in their mind.

- **Tactile Diaries**: Keeping collections of objects with distinct textures or weights that are associated with specific memories or people. These tactile diaries offer a tangible means of connecting with past experiences, relying on the sense of touch as a bridge to memory. I keep scrapbooks for most trips I go on, especially foreign holidays and long-distance multi-day walks. They have everything from feathers and seedheads to sheep's wool collected on barbed wire fencing. I often flip through my scrapbooks and can immediately take myself back to the time and place in my mind, through touch and sound alone.

- **Scent Journals**: Documenting life's moments through scents, whether it be perfumes, spices, or the natural odors of locations visited. This strategy turns scents into bookmarks for life's chapters. One embarrassing example I can recall here is from my early teenage years when I purposefully bought a can of my boyfriend's deodorant to remind me of him when we were not together. I remember it seeming weird to friends at the time and being mocked for it, but since learning that other people can bring people's faces to mind whenever they want, I guess this was simply my way of bringing him to mind. A quick squirt of "Insignia for Men" on my pillow and my teenage brain would be transported back to last week's slow dance at the youth club disco. It was the 80's deodorant of choice and mobile phones were not a thing back then so scrolling through imagery on a handheld device was still something only the crew of the Starship Enterprise were capable of.

- **Flavour Mapping**: Using the nuances of taste to anchor memories or emotions, such as associating different drinks or dishes with specific events, places, or timeframes. Ginger tea will always take me to a trip I took in 2014 with my Mum to Cambodia. I've never found another ginger tea like it, but now, any kind of ginger tea, fried rice, or Berocca soluble vitamins will always form part of my flavour map of that trip. Another example here is the tradition of reserving certain foods for specific events. For example, our family reserves scrambled eggs with smoked salmon for breakfast at Christmas or New Year's, not only ensuring they are kept special, but for me, this has forever attached those combined flavours to feelings of happiness and relaxation, family and downtime. I also fondly remember my very first trip to Africa when I stayed with friends in Zimbabwe and they included me in their family tradition of "mangoes and mealies" with sundowners on a local elevated landmark. The taste and texture of those fresh juicy mangoes and the satisfying crunch of those warm, buttery corn cobs will stay with me forever.

You may already, and very naturally, use many of these personal strategies to maximize the role of your other senses, but if not, try to make a conscious effort to think about how you observe and record events going forward and you may find that your memory can make many more associations than you think it can.

Chapter 4: Challenges and Coping Strategies

4.1 Daily Life

For anyone, a well-oiled routine is like the backbone of daily life, it's no different when you've got aphantasia, it's just we use different tools to keep everything running smoothly.

Without the ability to visualize in our heads, external tools become our best friends. Is this any different I wonder to someone with a functioning mind's eye? especially in today's hectic and fast-paced world? I can't say, but here is what it looks like for organized aphants;

- **Calendars Everywhere**: Digital or physical, calendars are our visual cue for what's coming. Syncing them across devices ensures we're always in the loop, no mental imagery is needed.

- **The Almighty Checklist**: There's a palpable satisfaction in ticking off tasks. Checklists not only guide our day but also provide a tangible record of our accomplishments. They are like breadcrumbs we leave ourselves; they guide us back when our mind can't map the way.

- **Note-Taking**: And when it comes to note-taking, we're not just jotting down thoughts—we're externalizing our brain's storage.

- **Digital Notepads**: Apps on our phones or computers are perfect for capturing thoughts on the go. They're searchable, which is a godsend for quickly retrieving information.

- **Physical Notebooks**: For many, the act of writing by hand aids in retention. Themed notebooks for different aspects of life, work, hobbies, and personal goals—keep everything compartmentalized.

- **Color-Coding**: Who needs to visualize when colours can do the heavy lifting? Assigning colours to different types of tasks or events simplifies organization and adds a dash of vibrancy to our planning.

- **Voice Memos**: Sometimes, speaking is faster than writing. A quick voice note can capture an idea more naturally than a hastily typed sentence.

I know my world would turn to chaos pretty quickly without the wealth of organizational apps, trackers, and chrome extensions I have installed on my various devices.

4.2 Memory Hacks: Techniques to Enhance Recall

Before we get into this, I feel I ought to confess that I have tried this countless times, and it simply doesn't work for me, however, other aphants swear by it, so I include it here as something that may work for you.

Building a Memory Palace

The 'method of loci', also known as the memory palace technique, might seem visual, but it's incredibly adaptable for those of us without a mind's eye. It's about associating information with specific locations or sequences in a familiar physical space, like your home. However, when the canvas of your mind's eye remains blank, this method demands a creative twist, turning to tactile and auditory cues instead of visual ones.

You can assign concepts or tasks to different rooms or objects within those rooms, and then "walk" through this space in your mind to recall them. The trick is to use spatial relationships and the familiarity of the environment as cues, rather than visualizing them.

The key to this adaptation is in spatial memory - the understanding of how things relate to each other in space, even if we can't "see" them in our minds. It taps into how we navigate the world daily, recalling the layout of our home or the sequence of turns to our favourite cafe, not through images but through a sense of knowing.

- **Choose Your Palace Wisely**: Start with a place you know like the back of your hand. This could be your home, workplace, or even a route you frequently travel. The familiarity breeds a map in your mind that doesn't require visual cues.

- **Anchor Points**: Instead of trying and failing to visualize objects in each room or location, focus instead on physical sensations or the sequence of movements. For instance, the feel of the doorknob as you enter, the sound of the floorboards creaking, or the smell of coffee in the kitchen can serve as potent anchors for placing the items you wish to remember.

- **Sensory Tags**: Attach each piece of information to a sensory experience. A fact you need to recall could be linked to the sound of a ticking clock or the texture of the carpet underfoot. These sensory tags act as cues, pulling forth the information when you mentally "walk" through your palace.

- **Narrative Walkthroughs**: Without trying to visualize, narrate a walkthrough of this space in your mind, stopping at each location to recall the piece of information associated with it.

The proof, as they say, is in the pudding. Numerous individuals with aphantasia have tailored the memory palace technique to great success, finding it a game-changer in both academic and professional settings, but like I say, it still eludes me, so don't feel too bad if it doesn't work for you either.

One student, preparing for a major exam, transformed their dorm room into a memory palace, associating key concepts with the feel of different textures around the room - the smooth wood of the desk, the rough fabric of the curtains, and so on. This tactile map led them to ace the exam, proving that visualization isn't the only path to stellar memory retention.

A professional, tasked with delivering a detailed presentation, used the route from their office to the conference room as a memory palace. Each turn and door became an anchor for different sections of the presentation, with the physical act of walking the route helping to cement the sequence and content in their mind.

Applications and Benefits

Beyond academic learning and professional presentations, it's a tool that enhances daily life, from remembering grocery lists to keeping track of important dates.

- **Academic Success**: Students find it an invaluable technique for mastering complex information, from historical timelines to the intricacies of human anatomy.

- **Professional Efficiency**: In the workplace, it's a blessing for memorizing the flow of meetings, key points of projects, or even the names and details of colleagues and clients.

- **Everyday Organization**: On a personal level, it simplifies life management, turning the abstract into something graspable, without the need for visual recall.

Verbal Encoding

Turning visual information into words or sounds involves describing scenes, objects, or concepts in detailed verbal terms, which can then be recalled more easily. For instance, instead of trying to picture a beach, aphants tend to think about the sensation of sand beneath our feet, the rhythm of the waves, and the warmth of the sun on our skin—all described in rich, descriptive language. This method leverages the linguistic parts of our brain to strengthen memory.

- **Daily Practice**: Start with something simple, like your morning routine, and narrate it to yourself in detail. Over time, this practice can help improve your ability to encode and recall information verbally.

- **Use Rhymes and Songs**: Adding rhythm or melody can make verbal information even more memorable. Create little jingles about things you want to remember, like a grocery list or a to-do list.

Repetition and Association

The saying "practice makes perfect" holds weight here, as repeating information solidifies it in our memory. But this goes beyond mere repetition. By linking new information to something already well-established in our minds, we create a web of associations that makes recall smoother and more reliable. For example, if you're trying to remember a new person's name, associate it with a familiar person or concept that shares some similarity, be it sound, meaning, or thematic connection.

- **Build Associations**: When introduced to new concepts, immediately link them to something familiar. It creates a mental "hook" for easier retrieval.

- **Scheduled Reviews**: Set times to review new information, gradually increasing intervals between reviews. This spaced repetition solidifies the memory.

4.3 Modern Support Tools

As well as the inspirational stories from others with aphantasia, modern technology has also thrown us a lifeline, offering apps and aids that can turn verbal descriptions into a clear picture, or at least, a well-defined map to guide us through. Here's a rundown of the tech tools designed to make life a bit easier for folks with aphantasia:

- **Voice Assistants**: Ever tried asking Siri, Alexa, or Google to remind you of an appointment or describe a recipe step-by-step? It's like having a personal assistant who's always on call, ready to provide information and timely prompts.

- **Text-to-Speech Apps**: Reading a lengthy article or a chapter from a book without visualizing the content can be taxing. Text-to-speech apps like NaturalReader or Voice Dream turn those words into audio, allowing you to absorb information through listening, which for many of us, is a more natural fit.

- **Note-Taking Software**: Evernote and Microsoft OneNote are game-changers, letting you organize your thoughts, lists, and reminders in a neatly structured digital format. They're especially handy for keeping track of details you might not visualize but need to remember.

Visualization Software

Just because we can't see it in our mind's eye doesn't mean we shy away from visuals. On the contrary, we lean into them in our external world, using technology and visual aids to bridge the gap.

- **Flowcharts and Diagrams**: For complex tasks or projects, laying out the steps visually can clarify what seems like a tangled process.

- **Mind Mapping Software**: Tools like MindMeister or Coggle help in organizing thoughts, planning projects, or brainstorming, offering a bird's eye view of where everything stands.

- **Video Tutorials**: When learning something new, video tutorials are invaluable. They provide the visual context we can't generate internally, making it easier to grasp concepts or follow along. YouTube has been a total game changer for me and is my go-to for any new craft skill or home DIY task that I need to get done.

Memory and Organization Apps: Keeping It All Together

Without the ability to visualize, keeping track of tasks, appointments, and even personal belongings can feel like juggling while blindfolded. Thankfully, there's an app for that. Actually, there are several:

- **Task Management**: Apps like Todoist or Trello lay out your tasks and projects in an easily navigable format. They're like digital to-do lists but better, allowing you to categorize, prioritize, and even share tasks with others.

- **Calendar Apps**: Google Calendar or Apple Calendar are life-savers for remembering appointments, birthdays, and events, with alerts and notifications to ensure you never miss a beat. Many sites now have downloadable calendars for upcoming sports competitions – I wouldn't be without it for planning my social life around the Six Nations rugby fixtures!

- **Location Trackers**: Ever forget where you put your keys? Tile and other Bluetooth trackers can be attached to items you frequently misplace, allowing you to locate them through an app. It's a simple solution that saves time and reduces frustration, especially when some helpful friend asks you to "retrace your steps" – yeah right, how exactly is that done?

Visualization Aids: Seeing Through Technology

While we might not create mental images the conventional way, technology provides alternative routes to "see". Virtual Reality (VR) and Augmented Reality (AR) are at the forefront of this, offering immersive experiences that don't require our minds to do the heavy lifting:

- **VR for Learning and Exploration**: Strap on a VR headset, and you can be transported to the ruins of ancient Rome or the depths of the ocean. It's a way to explore and learn about the world with a richness of detail that reading or traditional study can't match.

- **AR for Daily Assistance**: Apps like Google Lens allow you to point your phone's camera at an object to get information about it. It's a bit like having a visual search engine in your pocket, bridging the gap between the physical and the digital, and enhancing what you see with layers of context and information.

In the digital age, technology serves as a bridge, a tool, and a companion for those of us who don't think in pictures. It's a testament to human ingenuity, showing that even when our internal experiences differ, we can find common ground and shared solutions in the external, digital world.

Through apps and technologies designed to assist, enhance, and connect, we find ways to navigate, understand, and thrive in a world rich with imagery, even if we don't "see" it in the traditional sense.

4.4 Engaging the World Beyond Sight

In the last chapter, we looked at the possibility of sensory compensation. Now let's look at sensory exploration. Something I am a keen promoter of in my role as a safari camp guide and host. Not just to help aphants, but because I believe everyone can benefit from improving their mental and physical well-being using such techniques.

When visual imagery sits just out of reach, the world seems to respond by amplifying its other messages. It whispers in scents, sings in flavours, and dances under fingertips. This section is a celebration of those messages, a guide to tuning in more closely and discovering how rich life can be when experienced through all senses not just relying on sight.

Sensory Exploration

Consider for a moment the last meal that truly moved you. Was it just the taste, or was it the symphony of sensations — the aroma wafting through the air, the sizzling sounds from the kitchen, the warmth of the dish in your hands? This is sensory exploration: a deliberate deep dive into the world's subtler, often overlooked details. It's about noticing the way rain feels against your skin compared to the sensation of a warm shower or distinguishing each individual sound in a busy café. Something I learned to do quite well in the African bush was to isolate each individual bird call, I might not be good enough yet to name them all, but the act of stopping, listening, and counting how many different species I can hear, (and subsequently "voices" or individuals), is a lesson in mindfulness that I still practice today.

To enhance all your senses, (tactile, auditory, olfactory, and gustatory), consider these activities as your sensory playground:

- **Cooking**: Beyond taste, cooking engages all senses. Pay attention to the sound of ingredients sizzling, the aroma of spices heating, and the texture of dough as you knead. Cooking becomes not just about feeding the body but nourishing the soul.

- **Soundbites**: Spend an afternoon collecting sounds. Whether in nature or a bustling urban centre, record snippets of the world around you. Later, listen back and notice the layers and textures of each environment. Radio stations often run competitions too which ask the listener to identify the sound from a short clip played back over a few days – I wonder whether blind people or aphants are better at this than non-aphants or sighted people?

- **Blind Tasting**: Organize a tasting event where the focus is solely on flavour. With vision out of the equation, other aspects of the food — texture, temperature, and subtle taste nuances — come to the forefront.

- **Aromatic Journeys**: Create an 'aroma kit' with various essential oils, herbs, and spices. Regularly spend time with each scent, noting the emotions and memories they evoke. As a side bonus, I've heard that sniffing pine or peppermint oil can tell your appetite to stop craving snack foods during the day!

Sensory Training Techniques

Sharpening our senses allows us to experience the world in high definition. Here are techniques to sensitize and enhance our non-visual perceptions:

- **Mindful Eating**: Slow down during meals to notice the complexity of flavours and textures. It's not just about what you're eating but how each bite feels and tastes.

- **Texture Boards**: Create a board or a box filled with materials of varying textures. Regular interaction with these can heighten tactile awareness, making the sense of touch more discerning.

- **Focused Listening Sessions:** Dedicate time to listen to music or natural sounds with closed eyes, concentrating solely on the auditory experience. Try to pick out individual instruments or the subtlest sounds in the background.

The Richness of Sensory Experiences

Here are a few examples, picked from various social media groups and forums, that illuminate the diversity and richness of living a sensory-focussed life:

- A musician describes how losing their sight enhanced their ability to perceive music, noting nuances and layers they'd never appreciated before. For them, music isn't just heard; it's felt, resonating through every fiber of their being.

- A chef with aphantasia talks about how cooking is an intimate dance with ingredients, guided by scent, touch, and taste. They don't see dishes in their mind before creating them; they evolve, guided by the sensory feedback loop between the chef and their creations.

- An avid furniture flipper or up-cycler shares how their workshop is a sanctuary of colours and textures. Without a mental image of the final piece they are trying to create, they navigate through touch and trial, each fabric offering a unique sensory signature that guides their creations.

In a world that often prioritizes sight above all else, recognizing and celebrating the full spectrum of sensory experiences opens up new avenues of connection and enjoyment. It's a reminder that there's more than one way to perceive and appreciate the beauty around us. By engaging deeply with our senses, we not only compensate for the lack of visual imagery but also enrich our lives with experiences that are just as meaningful and vivid.

As we draw this exploration to a close, remember, that the world communicates in a language broader and more diverse than sight alone. And as we turn our attention to the next chapter, let's carry with us the knowledge that our experiences are not diminished by aphantasia.

4.5 Communication Strategies: Expressing the Inexpressible

Whilst it may be subtle, living with aphantasia introduces unique nuances into the art of communication, especially when the conversation turns to visual experiences. But fear not; there are avenues to bridge this gap, ensuring our interactions remain rich, engaging, and, most importantly, understood by all parties involved.

Descriptive Language

When the mind's eye doesn't paint pictures, words become our palette and brush. Here are a few ideas for how to make descriptive language work for you:

- **Sensory Details**: Focus on describing how things feel, sound, smell, and taste. This approach can often provide a more immersive description than visual details alone.

- **Analogies and Metaphors**: These are my "go-to's" when conveying complex ideas or images. By comparing the unfamiliar with something well-known, you can create a bridge of understanding.

- **Active Verbs**: Bring your descriptions to life with action. Instead of saying, "The cat is on the mat," try "The cat curls up on the mat, purring softly." It paints a more dynamic picture.

- **Precision**: Be as specific as possible. The devil is in the details, and these details can make your descriptions far more vivid and engaging.

Empathy and Patience in Conversations

Discussions about visual experiences can be frustrating at times and require mutual understanding and a little patience. It's about creating a space where everyone feels heard and respected, regardless of how they process information.

- **Clarify Without Judgment**: If you're having trouble grasping a visual description, ask for clarification in a way that's open and non-judgmental. Phrases like, "Can you describe how that looks in another way?" invite further explanation without implying a lack.

- **Share Your Perspective**: Don't shy away from explaining your experience of aphantasia. People often don't realize the diversity in mental processing, and your insight can be eye-opening.

- **Patience Is Key**: Whether you're trying to understand a visual explanation or conveying your non-visual experience, patience on both sides of the conversation helps. Remember, this is as much about learning from each other as it is about the topic at hand.

Creative Communication

Embracing creativity in how we communicate allows us to connect and share experiences in unique and meaningful ways.

- **Music and Sound**: Create playlists or soundscapes that convey emotions or themes you're discussing. As we've said, sounds can evoke a strong sense of place or mood, providing a common ground for shared understanding.

- **Writing**: Putting your thoughts down on paper lets you go deeper and add those subtle details that might get lost when you're talking. Whether it's writing poems, telling stories, or just jotting down your thoughts in a journal, like painting a clear picture with words for both you and whoever reads it.

- **Art and Visual Aids**: If you're working on a project or trying to convey an idea, collaborating with artists, or using visual aids can help bridge the gap. Diagrams, illustrations, or even simple sketches can convey what words might not. I find Pinterest boards are really useful for this.

- **Interactive Experiences**: Sometimes, actually doing stuff together can be a super effective way to get your point across. Like going on guided walks, getting your hands dirty in workshops, or doing activities together. It's way better than just talking about it because you're experiencing it firsthand.

It's about embracing the tools at our disposal, whether they be words, technology, or creative expression, to ensure that our ideas, experiences, and emotions are fully shared and understood.

4.6 Processing Feelings Without Visual Cues

Images often evoke strong emotions; with aphantasia, this means finding alternative ways to explore our emotional landscapes. As aphants, we can still evoke all those emotions, we just do it conceptually instead of visually.

Without the ability to "see" a sunny beach or a serene forest in our mind's eye, how do we tap into the emotions these images might evoke? The answer lies in focusing on the essence of the emotion itself, rather than the imagery usually associated with it. I can't speak for everyone of course, but here's how I believe we aphants do it:

- **Recalling the wider sensory experience**: Drawing upon the feelings associated with textures, sounds, or scents. The warmth of sunlight on your skin, the feeling of sand between your toes, the taste of the salty air, or the sound of waves crashing onto the shore can evoke emotions similar to, if not more powerful than, visual imagery.

- **Emotional Labelling**: Identifying and naming emotions as you experience them. This helps in understanding and processing feelings without needing to visualize a scenario.

- **Physical Awareness**: Sometimes, emotions manifest physically—a tight chest for anxiety, a fluttery stomach for excitement. Tuning into these physical sensations at the time helps us to record our emotional state and remember it.

Journaling and Verbal Expression

Words become our lifelines, a way to articulate the sea of emotions within. Here's why putting pen to paper or words into the air can be transformative:

- **Clarity and Insight**: Writing or speaking about your emotions helps in untangling them, providing clarity, and sometimes revealing underlying causes or solutions.

- **Emotional Release**: The act of expression is cathartic. It allows for an emotional release, a way to let go of what's been bottled up inside.

- **Memory Aid**: If you're like me and don't have any visuals to trigger past feelings, keeping written or spoken records can be a real eye-opener. They help us remember where we've been emotionally and how far we've come. I tend to write blogs, make voice recordings on my mobile phone, and occasionally video diaries of trips away. I have looked back on some of these recordings years later and have been blown away by the amount I have forgotten about the trip. But hearing my own voice describe in my own words how amazing or breathtaking something was, has been invaluable for me. I might not be able to picture the scene again, but I can see from my facial expressions or the sound of my voice at the time how I must have felt.

Support Systems

Many people go their whole lives not knowing they have aphantasia, so the argument for support systems can seem overkill. However just as ignorance is bliss, so knowledge is understanding. Support systems give us a safe space to share knowledge.

- **Seek Understanding**: Surround yourself with people who are willing to understand aphantasia and its impact on your emotional world. Educating friends and family can build deeper connections (unless you have close friends like mine who love the banter, in which case it opens up a whole new level of mickey-taking which leads to laughter but eventually yes, deeper connections).

- **Join Support Groups**: Engage with online or local support groups for individuals with aphantasia. These communities offer a space to share strategies, experiences, and support. We will discuss this further in the next chapter.

- **Professional Help**: If you are struggling, don't hesitate to seek help from therapists or counselors, especially those familiar with or open to learning about aphantasia. They can offer tailored strategies for emotional processing and support.

Chapter 5: Nurturing Connections

5.1 Aphantasia in Relationships

I debated with myself many times about whether to leave this section in or take it out. I've re-written it, changed the message, and researched it on forums and I am still undecided about whether or not aphantasia really has any noticeable effect on intimate relationships.

I am lucky enough to have known my partner since I was a teenager and we have been in a relationship for decades now. I didn't realize I had aphantasia until I was in my 40s, so we had managed just fine throughout our time together. But maybe that's because I believe I was probably born this way. The situation for people with *acquired* aphantasia can be hugely different. Mainly because they haven't had a lifetime of learning to adapt, but suddenly find themselves without a mind's eye, where previously they did. I believe this sudden change is disorientating, frustrating and I suspect quite unnerving. I don't remember a time when I could visualize in my mind, which makes me one of the lucky ones.

For many, being unable to conjure images in your mind has impacted intimate relationships in various ways. The main one I hear cited is not being able to visually recall shared memories or the inability to mentally visualize future scenarios together which creates a distance that can lead to frustration.

In my experience, understanding and open communication between partners helps to overcome *any* obstacles in intimate relationships, whether they are related to mind-blindness or whose turn it is to fold the laundry!

Just because I cannot "see" our past or our future as pictures in my mind, doesn't mean I cannot imagine or discuss it. All relationships have their quirks of course and ours is no different, but I don't see how my being able to conjure images in my head would impact our relationship positively or negatively. It just is what it is – but maybe that's because I don't know what I'm missing in terms of live-streaming the best bits of our past inside my mind!

Alternative Expressions of Love and Intimacy

Love and intimacy are multifaceted – it's my belief that they're not at all confined to shared visual experiences. They thrive on understanding, mutual respect, and finding unique ways to express affection, like those listed below;

- **Words Over Images**: Sometimes, a well-placed note, a heartfelt letter, or even a text message can convey deep affection and intimacy more profoundly than a thousand mental pictures.

- **Acts of Service**: Doing something meaningful for your partner, like brewing their favourite tea in the morning or taking care of a chore they dislike, speaks volumes of your love and care. I don't believe in the saying "treat others how you would want to be treated" because everyone is different. I believe in treating others how you know they would want to be treated, and if you don't know, just be respectful or ask!

- **Quality Time**: It's about being present, truly listening, and engaging with each other's world. Shared activities, deep conversations, and making new memories together can strengthen bonds beyond the visual.

- **Physical Touch**: A touch, a hug, or a kiss can communicate more love and intimacy than any mental picture could ever hope to convey.

Shared Memories

Memories are like the bookmarks of our relationships, but what if you can't picture them in your mind's eye? How do you keep those memories fresh and your story alive without visualizing them?

- **Shared Journals**: Keeping a journal of your experiences together, with entries from both of you, captures the essence of those moments in words. A lifelong friend and I keep a giant scrapbook of our times together, (visits, weekends away, and special events) which we swap ownership of, back and forth with each passing year. It's become one of my most treasured possessions.

- **Photo Albums with Captions**: Collect photos of your time together but add detailed captions describing how each moment felt, what made it special, and why it's worth remembering.

- **Audio and Video Memories**: Recording sounds or video clips from special occasions – a clip of laughter, a snippet of music from a dance, the atmosphere of a place that means a lot to you – these can be powerful memory triggers. These days, there are also some incredible and free online tools to turn your clips into mini-videos without too much effort – why not make the most of them? Your video creations don't have to be perfect, nor do they have to be shared with anyone else, but they make great talking points when you take a trip down memory lane together.

Understanding and Accommodation

The bedrock of any relationship is understanding and accommodation. I am a firmer believer that you choose the person you love, and then spend the rest of your days loving the person you chose. True partnership is a two-way street, requiring openness from both parties and when you both subscribe to this same way of thinking, then compromise is rarely needed.

- **Educate and Share**: Help your friend/partner understand what aphantasia is and how it affects you. This isn't just about the inability to visualize but also about how rich and deep your world is, experienced in different ways.

- **Patience and Support**: Patience goes a long way. There will be moments of disconnect, but with support and understanding, these can be transformed into opportunities for deeper connection.

- **Find Your Language**: Every relationship develops its own language of love and intimacy. For aphants, this language might lean more on verbal expression, tactile experiences, and shared activities. It's about finding what uniquely works for you and embracing it.

5.2 Family Dynamics: Explaining Aphantasia to Relatives

When the topic of aphantasia comes up at the dinner table or during a casual family gathering, you might notice raised eyebrows or puzzled looks. It's a concept that, until recently, remained under the radar. I've found that the raised eyebrows are usually because people who do see in their minds simply cannot comprehend that there are people who can't. But there are ways to shed light on what it means for you and how you can encourage others to offer their support.

Initiating Conversations

You will likely feel apprehensive before starting a conversation about aphantasia. You want to keep everyone on board without causing a stir. Try framing it around a specific instance that illustrates your experience. Maybe mention how, when everyone else describes "picturing" beloved memories or future dreams, your process feels different, more abstract. It's not about seeing with your mind's eye but understanding and feeling in vibrant detail. Lots of aphants use the term "conceptualize" instead of visualize. Because we don't have any issue thinking about things, we just don't *see* them.

- **Ease into It**: Begin with a simple question like, "You know how sometimes people say they can 'see' things in their mind? What's that like for you?" It can naturally lead to explaining how your experience differs.

- **Share Your Feelings**: Let them know why you're bringing this up. Whether it's seeking understanding, expressing a part of your identity, or just sharing something fascinating about human diversity, your reasons can guide the depth and direction of the conversation.

Educational Resources for Families

A little bit of homework can go a long way. There are now many resources out there designed to explain aphantasia for those unfamiliar with it. Before diving deep into discussions, you might share an article or two, a video, or a podcast as pre-reading/viewing. This will give everyone a base understanding, making the conversation smoother and more productive.

Activities for Connection

Finding common ground is key in any family dynamic – no one likes that awkward silence or forced conversation that feels unnatural. When visual imagination isn't a shared experience, doing activities that don't rely on it is essential. Choosing inclusive options ensures everyone can participate and increases the chances that everyone will enjoy it and want to do it again. It's about finding common ground where visual imagination isn't the focal point. Think about what engages the senses, sparks conversation, or requires teamwork. Here are a few suggestions;

- **Music and Concerts**: Enjoying live music together taps into our auditory senses, creating shared experiences that don't rely on visual cues. Discussing the songs, the emotions they evoke, or even the vibe of the venue afterward can enrich your connection.

- **Tasting Events**: Whether it's a wine tasting, a coffee cupping session, or a culinary tour, these activities engage the taste buds and provide a sensory-rich experience that everyone can relive afterward, although I would recommend taking it a bit easy at a whiskey tasting – I came a cropper once at an event in Zambia!

- **Crafting Workshops**: Engaging in crafts, from pottery to wood carving, focuses on tactile sensations and the joy of creating something tangible. These workshops offer a way to bond over the learning process and the items created, rather than visual outcomes. Times spent with friends that I find easiest to remember are when we've been on bushcraft courses, making bows and arrows, rustic chairs, or simple woodland spoons.

- **Storytelling Nights**: Hosting an evening where everyone shares campfire stories, whether personal tales or fictional narratives, cultivates a sense of closeness. Some of my most magical memories are of fireside recitals, accompanied by the crackle of burning logs, the warmth of the fire down my shins, and the distant call of owls in the night.

- **Cooking Together**: Recipes are a beautiful blend of structure and creativity, perfect for families to tackle together. Each person can take on a task, from reading the recipe out loud to measuring ingredients or stirring the pot. Friends and I love to camp, and a big part of each trip is cooking and eating together. Each couple will take charge of either a dish to bring along or a task during cooking like feeding the fire, turning the meat, or wrapping the baked potatoes. This division of tasks coming together to form a meal is what makes the whole thing a truly shared experience and all the more memorable for it.

- **Nature Walks**: Being outdoors, with the sounds of wildlife, the scent of trees, and the feel of different terrains underfoot, offers a sensory-rich experience that everyone can enjoy and discuss.

- **Board Games and Puzzles**: Choose games that rely more on strategy, wordplay, or teamwork rather than those that require visual imagination or visual memory.

Supporting Children with Aphantasia

For parents discovering their child might experience the world without visual imagery, the priority naturally becomes more about building an environment where this difference is accepted and embraced, and the child is not excluded or made to feel stupid. That said, for some, there is an argument for not treating the child any differently and letting their natural coping mechanisms kick in. After all, a large percentage of people with aphantasia manage just fine and spend their whole lives oblivious to any difference in brain wiring. If you feel the need to make accommodations, here are some of the suggestions made by the aphantasia community that can help;

- **Open Dialogue**: Encourage open and honest conversations about how your child experiences their thoughts and memories. Validate their experiences and remind them that there's no right or wrong way to think or imagine.

- **Focus on Strengths**: Highlight and nurture your child's strengths, whether in academia, creativity, or problem-solving. Aphantasia often comes with its own set of skills and perspectives that can be celebrated and developed.

- **Advocate at School**: Work with teachers to ensure they understand your child's learning style. Suggest alternative methods of instruction or assessment that align better with how your child processes information.

- **Explore Diverse Activities**: Encourage participation in a broad range of activities to discover what resonates with your child. Music, sports, writing, and science clubs can offer avenues for success and fulfillment beyond the visual.

5.3 Friendship and Nostalgia

Whilst I try hard to look to the future and not dwell on the past, I do love a good night of nostalgia; reminiscing about good times and funny things that have happened – these nights tend to reinforce friendships and bond us tighter together. However, most of my friends reminisce about past events with phrases like "Remember when we saw that incredible view from the top?" or "Remember the eyes of that lion staring straight at us when we went on safari?" whereas our contributions might lean more towards, "Remember how alive we felt standing there, it was so windy I thought we would take off!" or "and when he roared at night, we could feel the ground and the tent tremble!". It's a subtle shift, focusing on the essence of experiences rather than their visual snapshots. This approach doesn't dilute the richness of our interactions; instead, it adds a layer of depth, encouraging friends to explore memories and moments through a broader sensory spectrum.

Creating an environment of empathy and understanding among friends involves gently guiding them into our world. It's like inviting someone into your favourite book; you want them to appreciate the nuances and characters as much as you do. Here are some ways to increase understanding:

- **Share Your Perspective**: Conversations over coffee or during a quiet moment can be the perfect time to explain aphantasia. A simple, "You know, I experience things differently than most. I don't really 'see' images in my mind like others do," can open the door to deeper discussions.

- **Celebrate Diversity**: Highlight the beauty of experiencing the world in unique ways. Use examples like looking forward to your favourite dish at a restaurant without needing to picture the food itself but savoring the taste, smell, and texture, to illustrate how rich life can be without visual imagery.

- **Patiently Correct Misconceptions**: If a friend mistakenly believes aphantasia limits your ability to enjoy life or create, gently offer your perspective. Share how you've adapted and the unique ways you find joy and creativity in your life.

By building empathy and understanding, such deeply fulfilling and inclusive group activities are a reminder that friendships and social connections thrive not on shared visuals but on shared experiences and emotions, on understanding and accepting each other as we are.

5.4 Professional Interactions: Aphantasia at Work

I used to dread the quarterly meetings where our director gave his company vision speech for the software package we produced. He would always start with something like, "Picture this...," then launch into a spiel about how our software could be used in the future, what it would look like in situ, and how people would be able to use it in a more simplified manner with fancy dashboards and interactive camera feeds, and my colleagues would all nod in keen visualization while I was left sifting through words and feelings, a bit bewildered, desperately taking notes and writing bullet lists of what he planned to include in future versions. I can't imagine how this kind of thing would play out if you were an architect, or a designer of some kind – trying to take a client's ideas and put them down on paper?

It's clear to me now that succeeding at work with aphantasia requires its own playbook.

Workplace Disclosure

Choosing whether to share your aphantasia with colleagues and bosses is a bit like deciding to tell friends about a favourite hidden café. It could enrich your shared experience or change the dynamics in unforeseen ways. Let's look at both sides:

- **Pros**: Clearing the air can pave the way for understanding, especially in situations where visual tasks are on the table. It opens the door for adaptations that play to your strengths.

- **Cons**: There's always a risk of misconceptions. Some might mistakenly equate aphantasia with a lack of creativity or difficulty in strategic thinking.

If you decide to share, timing and context are your allies. A relaxed setting, perhaps during a one-on-one meeting or a casual team lunch, can set the right tone. You might say, "I approach tasks differently due to aphantasia, which means I don't visualize things in my mind the way most people do. But here's how I've turned it into my superpower..." This reframes the conversation around your unique strengths.

Adapting Work Processes

Tackling tasks and projects without the aid of mental imagery doesn't put us at a disadvantage; it simply means we take a different approach. Here are a few adaptations that can keep your workflow smooth and efficient:

- **Detailed Documentation**: Keep comprehensive notes and records. Not only does this help in keeping track of projects, but it also serves as a reference that you and your team can rely on.

- **Structured Planning**: Utilize tools and apps designed for project management. Platforms that offer a visual layout of tasks and timelines can help you organize your work without needing to picture it mentally.

- **Regular Check-Ins**: Schedule frequent updates with your team or supervisor. These meetings can serve as verbal walk-throughs of your projects, allowing you to discuss progress and hurdles without the need for visual aids.

Leveraging Unique Skills

The absence of mental imagery doesn't mean a lack of vision. In fact, it often means a more developed set of skills that are highly valuable in the workplace. Here's what you bring to the table:

- **Innovative Problem Solving**: Without preconceived visual biases, your approach to solving problems is uniquely outside the box. You're likely to come up with solutions that others might not consider.

- **Attention to Detail**: Since you rely more on facts and information than on imagery, you're likely to catch details others might miss. This makes you an invaluable asset in roles that require precision, accuracy, and attention to detail.

- **Strong Verbal and Written Communication**: Expressing thoughts and ideas without the crutch of visualization hones your communication skills, making you a clear and effective speaker and writer.

- **Adaptability**: Constantly finding ways to adapt to a visually oriented world makes you incredibly resilient and flexible – traits that are gold in the fast-paced professional realm. I appreciate that this might not ring true for those with recently acquired aphantasia.

Highlighting these skills during performance reviews or project discussions can shift the focus from how you're different to how you're an asset.

Seeking Accommodations

I am left-handed and whilst it irritates the hell out of me that I live in a predominantly right-handed world (that's a whole other book), I don't consider lefthandedness to be a disability and therefore don't feel that accommodations need to be made for me. I feel the same way about aphantasia. Yes, some things are irritating, but for the most part, I cope just fine and don't feel the need for any special treatment at work, but I realize this is not true for all.

Just as physical workspaces are adapted for physical needs, the cognitive work environment can also be adjusted to suit different ways of processing information. So if you feel that certain accommodations could enhance your productivity, here's how to advocate for them:

- **Identify Your Needs**: Before approaching HR or your supervisor, have a clear idea of what accommodations would help you. Whether it's access to specific software, permission to record meetings for later review, or additional time for tasks that require visualization, knowing what you need is the first step.

- **Prepare Your Case**: Gather evidence on how these accommodations would benefit not just you but your team or company. Highlight how they play to your strengths and contribute to your productivity.

- **Focus on Solutions**: Frame your request around solutions. Instead of emphasizing the challenges of aphantasia, focus on how the accommodations you're seeking are tools to unlock your full potential.

Dealing with the professional world wired as an aphant is not about overcoming a shortfall; it's about playing a different game – one where your unique approach, skills, and strategies lead you to success. By understanding how to disclose and discuss aphantasia, adapting your work processes, leveraging your distinct skills, and maybe seeking the accommodations you need, you're not just fitting into the workplace; you're redefining what it means to be an invaluable asset to your team and organization.

5.5 Building a Support Network: Community and Belonging

We've touched on this already in previous chapters, so let's delve a little deeper into what support really means and what it can do for you.

In the kaleidoscope of human experience, finding others who reflect your unique patterns can transform the way you see yourself. For aphants with our newly created label, the quest for connection leads us down a road not yet traveled by many. Yet, it's along this path that we discover communities brimming with familiar stories, new ideas and true empathy.

Finding Support Groups

Finding support groups and communities tailored to aphantasia is relatively straightforward in today's digital age. Start with a simple internet search, but don't stop there; reach out, engage, ask questions, and introduce yourself. Many find that these communities are more than willing to welcome new members, offering advice and sharing stories right from the start.

- Look for forums and websites specifically centered around aphantasia; they often host Q&A sessions and provide a plethora of resources. Aphant.asia and Reddit's r/Aphantasia are bustling with discussions, advice, and shared stories from individuals all over the globe. It's reassuring to know that even though our experiences are unique, we're not alone in them.

- Social media platforms can be goldmines for finding groups and pages dedicated to aphantasia. Facebook has numerous groups dedicated to aphantasia, where members share everything from scientific research to personal anecdotes. These groups are a great way to connect, ask questions, and take part in citizen science polls to gather new information.

- Don't overlook the power of hashtags on platforms like X and Instagram to discover content related to aphantasia and connect with individuals who share your experiences. Hashtags may have fallen out of favour, but there are still a huge number of them out there in the social space, waiting to direct you toward support and like-minded communities.

- Video Channels: YouTube hosts channels that delve into aphantasia, offering insights, interviews, and tips. It's a visual (ironically) and engaging way to learn more about the condition and how to manage it.

The Role of Support in Coping

Finding out you have aphantasia is a curveball for sure, but here's where the strength of a community becomes evident. Sharing your experiences with others who truly understand can lighten your load, making any obstacles you face seem less daunting. And by obstacles I mean all the questions that come up, all the comparisons you make to find out where you sit on the scale, and all the failed attempts you make to "see" something in your mind. It's about more than just venting frustrations; it's about discovering you're not alone, learning from others' coping strategies, and even finding humour in the shared quirks of aphantasia.

I love my friends dearly and am lucky enough to be able to talk to them about anything, including aphantasia, but because they all see perfectly clearly in their minds eyes, they are unable to truly understand what it's like. Scrolling posts on social media support groups plugs that gap for me;

- Hearing how others explain aphantasia to friends, family, and colleagues gives me new ideas for conversations in my own life.

- In these communities, tips for handling daily tasks, creative endeavors, and emotional expression flow freely, offering practical support.

- Simply knowing there are others out there who 'get it' can be a tremendous source of emotional relief and validation.

Creating Spaces for Sharing

While online communities offer a fantastic starting point, there's something irreplaceable about connecting in person – something it seems we all do less and less of since the pandemic. So why not be the one who initiates a local meetup? or creates a local interest group for individuals with aphantasia? Turn those virtual connections into a physical support network. Libraries, community centers, or even cozy cafes can serve as gathering spots where experiences and strategies can be shared face-to-face.

Benefits of Belonging

If you are struggling with feelings of isolation, FOMO, frustration, or simply not coping with aphantasia for whatever reason, the emotional and psychological uplift that comes from belonging to a community that understands and shares your experience will be of great benefit. Like finding your tribe, a group of people who speak your language in a world that often feels like it's speaking another.

As we move forward, let's carry with us the knowledge that our differences don't just set us apart—they draw us together.

Chapter 6: Advantages and Unique Perspectives

6.1 Rethinking Creativity

Imagine sitting down to solve a puzzle, but instead of relying on the picture on the box, you dive straight into connecting pieces by their shape and fit. It's a different approach, sure, but one that might just lead to a more intricate understanding of how the pieces relate. Without the ability to pre-visualize the finished puzzle, the process becomes one of exploration, discovery, and a deeper engagement with the material at hand. Creativity, then, isn't about reproducing images stored in the mental vault; it's about forging new connections, tapping into sensory experiences, and bringing to life something that didn't exist before.

Creative Solutions Without Visuals

Think about the last time you faced a tricky problem. Where did the solution come from? For someone without aphantasia, it might have involved visualizing various outcomes. But for those of us on the aphantasic spectrum, problem-solving takes a different route. It's less about seeing the end goal and more about feeling our way through the process, step by step. This tactile approach to creativity and problem-solving can lead to unique and innovative solutions. It's the difference between following a recipe to the letter and cooking by taste; both methods produce delicious results, but the latter relies on a more intuitive, and perhaps more creative, process.

Consider a fashion designer with aphantasia. Instead of starting with a clear image in their head, they might play directly with shapes, colours, and textures on their design software, experimenting and iterating in real-time. This hands-on, exploratory approach can lead to designs that are fresh and unexpected, precisely because they weren't preconceived.

Innovative Artistic Expressions

When our usual paths for creativity are changed, new ways of expressing ourselves emerge, often surprising even the creators themselves. Artists with aphantasia add to the diversity of the art world, proving that imagination isn't limited to visual imagery.

Expanding the Definition of Creativity

What does creativity actually mean? Creativity is not just painting a picture or sculpting a statue; it's solving problems, it's innovation, it's finding new ways to express an old idea. It's about the impact, the emotion, and the connection that creative work enables. Aphantasia, far from being a barrier to creativity, is simply a different starting point.

It's not just about what you can see with your eyes closed; it's about what you can make others feel, think, and understand.

6.2 Problem-Solving Skills: A Different Approach

Analytical Strengths

Without the visual noise that often accompanies the early stages of tackling a problem, those of us with aphantasia find our attention undivided, honed in on the task at hand. This lack of visual distractions doesn't just clear the cognitive runway for analytical thinking; it enhances it. We tend to notice patterns, inconsistencies, and details that might escape others. It's like reading a book and focusing purely on the narrative's structure, themes, and nuances without being swayed by the author's envisioned scenery or what the characters look like.

- **Precision in Detail**: With a mind less cluttered by preconceived visual notions, we're adept at zeroing in on the minutiae of a problem, often leading to more precise and thorough analysis.

- **Pattern Recognition**: Patterns emerge more starkly when you're not distracted by imagery. This skill is invaluable in fields like data analysis, coding, or even strategic planning, where recognizing and predicting patterns can lead to breakthrough solutions.

Alternative Strategies

Since the conventional route of visualizing solutions isn't an option, other ways of figuring things out start popping up. These methods, based on logic and step-by-step thinking, give us a clear path to tackle tricky problems.

- **Sequential Breakdown**: Approaching a problem step by step, focusing on how tasks logically connect, helps us really get what's going on, and often shows us problems before they get out of hand.

- **Logic-Based Frameworks**: Utilizing frameworks like SWOT (Strengths, Weaknesses, Opportunities, Threats) analysis or the Eisenhower Matrix for decision-making relies on logic rather than just going with your gut or relying on visuals.

Real-World Applications

The real-world applications of these problem-solving skills are vast and can make a big impact. Here are a few examples of where aphants typically thrive and innovate;

- **Software Development**: Coding is a language all its own, requiring a deep understanding of logic, structure, and the ability to foresee how different parts of a program interact. The aphantasic mind, adept at tackling complexities without visual aids, often excels in this environment.

- **Research and Analytics**: In roles that require sifting through data to extract meaningful insights, the ability to focus intensely on the information at hand, without being swayed by visual biases, can lead to more objective and comprehensive analysis.

- **Strategic Planning**: Creating plans for businesses or projects when you're not tied down by preconceived images, means you're free to think more creatively and adapt your plans as needed. You can be fluid. This flexibility often leads to thinking outside the box and coming up with innovative strategies that might not have been considered otherwise.

The Role of Collaboration

When diverse minds come together, the potential for innovation multiplies. Collaborative projects that blend different cognitive styles, including those with and without a mind's eye, are breeding grounds for groundbreaking ideas;

- **Balanced Abilities:** In a team, someone with aphantasia, who's great at analyzing details, can balance out the big-picture thinking and visual creativity of others. This mix helps the team tackle problems from all angles and come up with solid solutions.

- **Creative Results:** Projects that welcome input from different viewpoints tend to come up with more innovative ideas. They tap into a wider range of thoughts and ways to solve problems, which leads to more creative outcomes.

- **Better Communication:** Being part of diverse teams can also make you better at communicating. You get good at explaining your ideas in ways that everyone on the team can understand, even if they think differently.

From this perspective, aphantasia isn't a drawback at all. Instead, it promotes a careful, detail-focused method that, when teamed up with the visual and imaginative skills of others, can result in solutions that are both effective and creative.

6.3 Aphantasia and Mindfulness

Meditation

Why exactly is meditation so difficult for aphants? well for most of us, it is because guided meditations tend to be visual. They often start with something like "Imagine you are lying on a beach..." which we do conceptually; we feel the warmth of the sun on our faces, the breeze in our hair, and the sand beneath our feet. We hear the rhythmic crashing of waves and the calling of gulls high above us. But if the guiding voice then starts to take us on a visual journey, using lots of visual description, it becomes distracting and frankly quite annoying. The effort involved in conceptually trying to create the environment in our head is the complete opposite of clearing your mind. It's stressful and not in any way relaxing!

That said, without the constant stream of visual thoughts, aphants can often be more anchored in the immediate — centered on being fully present and engaged with the here and now – so forms of meditation that center around focussing on something with your eyes open are much more beneficial. Like finding a quiet spot, maybe a garden or park, and observing the smaller things around you. The ants crossing the path, flies feeding on flowers, bees buzzing from bloom to bloom. Revisiting the same "sit-spot" for ten minutes a day can become surprisingly addictive and rewarding, not to mention calming and de-stressing.

Don't give up on guided meditation though, as some forms can be successfully relaxing, they just need to take on a more sensory style. Here are some meditation examples that can work well for aphants;

- **Breath Focus**: Concentrate on the rhythm of your breath, and the way your chest rises and falls. The route of the air as it makes its way down to your lungs and diaphragm. It's a simple yet profound way to anchor yourself in the present moment and of course, can be done anywhere at any time. Sometimes I switch from air to blood and trace the circulatory route that my blood flows through my body, from my heart out to all my organs and limbs and back again.

- **Body Scans**: Progressively tune into each part of your body, acknowledging sensations without judgment. This practice heightens bodily awareness and creates a deep sense of relaxation. Notice where each body part comes into contact with the floor, the chair, or other objects depending on where you are, how does each muscle feel? each bone? each joint?

- **Audio Meditations**: Listen to guided meditations that emphasize sensory experiences or the repetition of verbal mantras. Many people find humming a sound whilst letting out a long exhale very calming as they not only feel the vibrations of each note but also hear any changes in tone or tempo. I used to do this as a kid, taking in a large breath, and then as if at the doctor's surgery, with mouth open, I would say "aaaah" letting it out as slowly as I possibly could till eventually only a single voicebox vibration at a time escaped my throat – admittedly I looked odd, sounded even odder, and was probably labeled a bit bonkers by my parents, but it soothed me a lot as a child. I was 100% focused on controlling my exhale, the speed, the volume, the tone, and the amount of air I had left.

- **Mindful Listening**: Engage in active listening exercises, focusing fully on the sounds around you, whether it's music, nature, or the hum of city life. Notice the layers, the changes, and how it feels to truly listen. I find counting or identifying the unique sources of sounds also quite meditative and challenge myself to not stop until I have identified at least twenty. Other times I might start with the sounds closest to me, like my heartbeat or breathing, and work outwards, eventually identifying the sounds furthest away from me.

- **Tactile Awareness**: Spend a few minutes each day focusing on tactile sensations. This could be the feel of different textures, the temperature of objects, or even the sensation of your own breath against your hand.

Our experience reminds us that mindfulness isn't about escaping to an inner visual sanctuary; it's about fully immersing ourselves in the reality of the moment, finding beauty and peace in the tangible and the true.

Reduced Anxiety from Visualization

It's well-documented that distressing mental images can amplify feelings of anxiety. For some, the lack of these images can act as a buffer. While we're certainly not immune to worry or stress, the absence of visual flashbacks or foreboding projections means our anxiety isn't compounded by distressing pictures. Note: This does not mean aphants are immune to suffering PTSD.

- **Handling Stress**: When faced with stress, our coping strategies lean more towards dealing with tangible issues rather than battling the phantoms of 'what-ifs' that visualization might conjure.

- **Processing Emotions**: Emotional processing for us might involve more direct engagement with the feelings themselves, as opposed to getting lost in a cycle of visualizing worst-case scenarios.

Enhanced Focus

Picture (figuratively, of course) trying to concentrate in a room where a TV is constantly flickering images. For those who visualize, particularly those with hyperphantasia, mental imagery can often be this unwelcome distraction. For aphants though, the screen is blank, allowing for an undivided focus on the task at hand. This enhanced concentration isn't just beneficial for productivity; it shapes how we learn, work, and even engage in our hobbies and interests.

- **Deep Work**: With fewer internal visual distractions, we might find it easier to enter a state of flow, fully immersing ourselves in complex tasks or creative endeavors.

- **Learning and Memory**: Our methods of learning and remembering information are tailored to our non-visual experience, often relying on structured information and logical sequencing, which can lead to a more focused and efficient study process.

6.4 Success Stories: Thriving with Aphantasia

In the world of aphantasia, many people haven't just adjusted to their unique way of experiencing the world—they've excelled in their fields. This section celebrates those who've turned what some might see as a limitation into their greatest strength. Their stories inspire and guide others living life with aphantasia.

Here are a few notable people who have publicly discussed having aphantasia:

- Blake Ross - Ross is known for co-creating the web browser Mozilla Firefox. He wrote an essay in 2015 titled "Aphantasia: How It Feels to Be Blind In Your Mind," where he shared his personal experience with aphantasia. The essay was published on his personal blog, and it gained significant attention and discussion in various media outlets.

- Ed Catmull - Catmull is a co-founder of Pixar Animation Studios and a computer scientist. He has spoken publicly about his own experience with aphantasia in interviews and articles. While specific sources may vary, he has discussed his condition in various contexts related to creativity, innovation, and his work in animation.

- Craig Venter - Venter is a biologist and entrepreneur who played a pivotal role in sequencing the human genome. He has mentioned having aphantasia in interviews. One notable interview where he discussed it was with BBC Radio 4's "Inside Science" program in 2016.

- Ben Folds - Folds is a musician known for his work as a singer-songwriter and pianist. He has openly talked about his experience with aphantasia in interviews, podcasts, and even in his music. One notable instance is his interview with NPR's "All Things Considered," where he discussed his song "Picture Window" and how it relates to his aphantasia.

These individuals have helped raise awareness about aphantasia by sharing their personal experiences with the condition.

Personal Triumphs

The narratives of personal achievement among those with aphantasia are as varied as they are inspiring, you only need to spend a little time perusing an Aphantasia-focussed social media group; There's the story of a marathon runner who, unable to visualize the finish line, focuses instead on the rhythm of their breath and the feel of the pavement underfoot, finding a meditative state that propels them forward. Then there's the entrepreneur who, in the absence of mental imagery, develops a keen ability to listen and adapt, leading their tech startup to innovate solutions that disrupt traditional markets.

A common theme emerges; success is not about the ability to see with the mind's eye but about the resilience, adaptability, and unique perspective each person brings to their endeavors.

A Celebrated chef uses their heightened sense of taste and smell to create dishes that earn accolades for their innovative flavours and textures, proving that culinary artistry isn't confined to visual presentation.

An acclaimed author, known for their richly detailed narratives, crafts worlds that captivate readers, drawing on a deep understanding of character emotion and human interaction rather than visual descriptions.

Unique Career Paths

The career trajectories of those with aphantasia often highlight how thinking differently can be a significant asset in professional environments. For instance, a forensic analyst excels in their field, relying on meticulous attention to detail and a methodical approach untouched by preconceived visual biases. This ability to focus on the facts with unparalleled clarity leads to breakthroughs in cases that had stumped others for years.

Similarly, a software engineer develops a groundbreaking coding language that simplifies complex concepts into intuitive commands, making programming accessible to a wider audience. Their success stems from a unique approach to problem-solving, untethered by the constraints of visual thinking, showcasing the boundless potential of aphantasic innovation.

In the realm of education, a teacher renowned for their engaging and inclusive classroom strategies creates a learning environment where every student feels seen, understood, and inspired. Their methods, refined through an understanding of diverse cognitive experiences, including aphantasia, becomes a model for educators worldwide.

A music producer, blending sounds in ways that resonate on a deep emotional level, achieves international fame. Their work, celebrated for its originality and depth, transcends the need for visual imagery, connecting with listeners through the universal language of music.

A scientist, tackling the challenge of explaining complex concepts without relying on visual aids, turns to analogies and real-world examples. This approach not only makes their work accessible to a broader audience but also garners acclaim for its clarity and ingenuity.

The list goes on; a filmmaker, creating narratives that touch on the human experience in profoundly moving ways, gains recognition for their work's emotional depth and complexity. Their storytelling, unencumbered by traditional visual scripting, resonates with audiences for its authenticity and innovation.

A public speaker, sharing their journey with aphantasia, becomes a source of encouragement and enlightenment. Through workshops and talks, they provide tools and strategies for others with aphantasia.

The sheer number of success stories within the aphantasia community highlights a vital truth: there are countless paths to success, each as unique as the individuals who walk them and although more research needs to be done on acquired aphantasia, it's clear to me that being mind blind from birth is no more a hindrance than lefthandedness.

Chapter 7: A Global Perspective

7.1 Cultural Variations Around the World

Imagine, if you will (and I mean that quite figuratively), stepping into a room where everyone is discussing the latest blockbuster movie, describing in vivid detail the breathtaking stunts, the dramatic landscapes, and the authentic costumes. Now, picture yourself (again, figuratively) not being able to conjure up those images, trying to grasp the essence of their excitement through the emotions in their voices, the enthusiasm in their gestures, and perhaps the detailed plot they outline. This scenario is a regular occurrence for people who are mind blind.

From the bustling streets of Tokyo to the serene landscapes of the Scottish Highlands, the ways in which people understand, accept, and support aphantasia vary enormously. This chapter takes us across continents and cultures to explore how aphantasia plays out within global societies.

Cultural Interpretations

Across the world, especially in societies with a strong emphasis on oral traditions and storytelling, aphantasia might not even be seen as a "thing", because the main focus is on telling stories through the rhythm of words and the emotions they evoke, rather than the ability to visualize them. Contrast this with highly visual cultures, where imagery, art, and visual symbols play a central role in communication and entertainment, and the experience of aphantasia might be more challenging.

Global Prevalence

Determining how widespread aphantasia is across different regions and cultures is tricky. Research is still in its infancy, and most studies are conducted in Western countries, with English-speaking participants. This leaves a significant gap in our understanding of aphantasia's prevalence worldwide. However, initial findings suggest that aphantasia, and its counterpart, Hyperphantasia (the ability to create highly vivid mental images), exist across all cultures and societies, though the rates may vary.

Cultural Stigmas

The degree of stigma or acceptance surrounding aphantasia also varies greatly from one culture to another. In some places, the lack of mental imagery might be met with skepticism or disbelief, viewed as a quirk or oddity. In others, it might be accepted as just another way of thinking, no more remarkable than being left-handed. The key factor seems to be how much value a culture places on visual thinking and creativity. Communities that prize innovation and cognitive diversity tend to be more accepting, while those that hold traditional views of intelligence and learning might view aphantasia more negatively.

For example, in tech-savvy societies where problem-solving and innovative thinking are highly valued, individuals with aphantasia might be celebrated for their unique approach to challenges. Conversely, in regions where education and intelligence are measured by rote memory and the ability to regurgitate information visually, the condition might be seen as a significant barrier.

Cultural Support Systems

Life with aphantasia can be smoother in cultures that offer robust support systems. These can take many forms, from educational resources tailored to different learning styles to community groups and online platforms. In countries with a strong emphasis on mental health and neurodiversity, resources might be more readily available, including counseling services, educational accommodations, and advocacy groups.

On the flip side, in places where awareness of aphantasia is low, individuals might find themselves forging their own paths, creating informal support networks, and relying on international online communities for information and camaraderie. The rise of social media and global connectivity has been a blessing in this regard, allowing people from all corners of the world to connect, share their stories, and offer each other support.

7.2 Language and Perception

Words do more than just pass along information; they shape our reality, influencing how we see things, feel, and interact with the world around us. In the world of aphantasia, the language we use and the terms we choose are incredibly important. Consider the term "aphantasia" itself, which you may remember is coined from the Greek words meaning "without" and "fantasy" – implying a lack or absence.

For many people in today's society, this terminology creates huge debate, but of course, it didn't back when the label was created – the world is changing, and it is changing at an alarming rate. At times, I find it a struggle to keep pace with what terms can and cannot be used in all aspects of life, not just those related to neurodiversity (another word that didn't exist when I was born!)..... but back to the point.... I get it, words like "mind-blindness", or "non-imagery" can emphasize what is missing rather than the unique ways in which people with aphantasia interpret the world, so I understand why they might be considered by some to be inappropriate. The challenge is to find language that accurately reflects the condition without casting it in a negative light, but at the same time is easy for everyone to grasp and accurately describes the condition.

I was born in the 70's, so I am used to calling a spade a spade. If the term "mind-blindness" fits the bill then I don't see any harm in using it. People can choose how they respond to labels and you can either be offended by it, or you can accept that it's simply a term that is easier to understand than a fancy term that may or may not be more inclusive and less negative. I begrudge being pigeon-holed at all and I'm not a fan of being labeled, but if the badge fits? My mind *is* blind, and let's be honest, mind-blind is far easier to say than "aphantasia"!

7.3 Global Approaches to Learning

As we touched on in Chapter 2, education can present a unique set of hurdles for individuals with aphantasia. The traditional classroom, with its reliance on visual aids and imagery-based learning techniques, isn't always the friendliest environment for those who experience the world differently. However, across the globe, innovative educational practices are emerging, reshaping the learning landscape to be more inclusive and accommodating for all minds.

Educational Challenges

In classrooms around the world, from Canada to Korea, students with aphantasia often face challenges. Traditional teaching techniques, like imagining historical events or mentally manipulating shapes, can seem daunting or even impossible for them. These methods not only hinder their understanding of visual subjects but also make it harder for them to participate in class discussions and stay engaged. Additionally, assessments that cater to visual learners—like exams requiring detailed visualizations—can make these students feel even more isolated and put them at a disadvantage.

Innovative Educational Practices

Around the world, educators are pioneering methods to bridge the gap, ensuring every student has the tools they need to thrive:

- In Finland, known for its progressive educational system, teachers are incorporating multisensory learning experiences. For instance, history lessons might include handling replicas of artifacts or listening to soundscapes that evoke a particular period, providing students with aphantasia a more tangible connection to the material.

- In Brazil, some schools are experimenting with role-play and storytelling as methods to teach literature and social sciences. This approach allows students to engage with content in an experiential way, moving beyond the need for mental imagery to grasp complex themes and narratives.

- In Australia, a movement toward personalized learning plans includes software that adapts to each student's learning style. For those with aphantasia, this might mean a focus on textual information and auditory explanations, with options to demonstrate understanding through written or spoken assignments rather than visual projects.

- Singapore, with its strong emphasis on technology in education, is leading the way in developing apps that cater to non-visual learners. These tools convert visual data into formats that can be understood through other sensory inputs, making subjects like geometry or chemistry more accessible to students with aphantasia.

Global Advocacy for Inclusion

The push for inclusive education is gaining momentum on the international stage. Organizations dedicated to neurodiversity are advocating for systemic changes that recognize and support the full spectrum of cognitive experiences, including aphantasia. These efforts are multifaceted, ranging from lobbying for policy changes to providing resources for teachers who wish to make their classrooms more accessible.

Learning from Each Other

The global community offers a wealth of ideas and approaches for supporting learners with aphantasia. International conferences on education and neurodiversity have become hubs for sharing knowledge and strategies. Educators from diverse backgrounds come together to share their experiences, successes, and obstacles, creating a shared wisdom that knows no boundaries.

Online platforms and forums serve as another vibrant arena for exchange, where teachers post lesson plans, activities, and assessments designed with aphantasia in mind, inviting feedback and suggestions from peers worldwide.

These interactions underline an important fact: diversity is our strength. By embracing a variety of experiences and methods, the education community can create environments where every student, no matter what way their brain is wired, can thrive and succeed.

7.4 Aphantasia and Travel

Travel is something I have been naturally drawn to all my life and have been lucky enough to visit an incredible number of countries both through work and on personal holidays. Traveling broadens our horizons, pushes our comfort zones, and offers a wealth of experiences. From the bustling markets of Marrakech to the serene silence of a Norwegian fjord, these journeys offer a unique way to connect with the world, grounding us in the moment and amplifying our sensory adventures.

Thankfully, in order for any of us to imagine what our trip will be like and to get that pre-trip anticipation we all know and love, we only need to get onto Google, and within a few clicks we can be shown a thousand images of our chosen location, read other people's blogs, photos, and reels. Then, when we arrive at our destination, the focus shifts from visual anticipation to sensory recording; the sound of a tropical forest after dark, the smell of street food in a lively market, and the foreign language surrounding us, all become strong memories of our travels. We immerse ourselves in the richness of now, letting the textures, sounds, and smells paint a picture of the world, and of course we usually take a million photos and videos to record the experience for sharing and give us the ability to relive it when we get home. But travel for aphants can also present a few obstacles. Let's look at a couple of the more obvious ones.

Navigational Strategies

Finding your way around new places is usually no different for aphants than it is for neurotypical people, but without a phone signal or Wi-Fi, it can often require a bit of creativity and some handy tools. Here are a few strategies that prove invaluable if you find yourself in an "off-grid" location:

- **Downloadable Maps and Apps**: Digital maps and offline sat nav is a godsend, providing real-time orientation and directions. Look for apps that offer auditory directions or haptic feedback.

- **Landmark Method**: Instead of trying to picture routes in your mind, focus on identifying unique landmarks. A distinctive building, a colourful mural, or a specific scent can serve as markers to guide your exploration.

- **Travel Journals**: Keeping a travel journal with you where you note down directions, underground stations, sensory cues, and personal reflections acts as a tangible record of your journey and can be a lifesaver when it's time to return to your accommodation.

Cultural Sensitivity

As we move through different cultures, sensitivity to local perceptions of aphantasia becomes hazy; not every culture understands or acknowledges the concept, which can lead to interesting conversations. So, if you choose to discuss aphantasia, frame it as a personal cognitive trait rather than a universal norm. This invites a respectful exchange of ideas and experiences.

Engage with locals to understand their perspectives on imagination and creativity. This can offer you a deeper understanding of the cultural context and enrich your travel experiences.

Global Awareness Campaigns

Around the world, efforts are underway to make travel and tourism more inclusive for all neurodivergents. These campaigns aim to educate the travel industry about cognitive diversity, encouraging the development of experiences that cater to all travelers. From hotels offering sensory-rich descriptions of their amenities to tour guides trained in delivering multi-sensory tours, the landscape of travel is slowly but surely becoming more enriched and less focused on the visual. These initiatives not only benefit those with recognized neurodivergent disabilities but can also enhance the travel experience for aphants and visual thinkers alike.

Chapter 8: Acceptance and Empowerment

8.1 Embracing Your Mind's Unique Landscape

Imagine you're at a concert, but instead of using your eyes to commit the event to memory, you're asked to record the experience and the music through vibrations, the scent of the crowd, and the taste of the air. For someone with aphantasia, this is the default mode; it's about tuning into a different frequency of experience so that when we relive it in our minds afterward, it's as vivid as it can be.

If you're struggling with aphantasia, this chapter is about flipping the script, from just understanding and accepting it to celebrating the unique way your brain functions.

Understanding as the First Step

We've spent a great deal of this book increasing our understanding of the unique way in which our brain operates and trying not to focus on what it lacks. Simply put, if most brains are like smartphones that store images and videos, ours is more like a top-notch podcast app, rich with sounds, dialogues, and music. Recognizing this doesn't mean settling; it means starting from a place of strength. Knowing the ins and outs of your mental processes is the first step towards acceptance.

- Keep a daily log for a week or two, jotting down how you experience memories, ideas, and dreams. Remember, this isn't about what you can't do; it's about mapping out your thoughts in all their non-visual glory.

- Chat with others who have aphantasia. Notice how their experiences resonate with or differ from yours.

Neurodiversity and Its Strengths

Neurodiversity is a game-changer in how we think about mental landscapes. This concept champions the idea that neurological differences like autism, ADHD, and yes, aphantasia, aren't defects but variations. Embracing neurodiversity means recognizing that aphantasia brings its own set of strengths to the table. Maybe you're a wizard with words, crafting narratives that others can only dream of. Or perhaps your problem-solving skills are off the charts, seeing solutions where others see dead ends.

Reflect on moments when your unique way of thinking gave you an edge. Was it a time when you outperformed in a strategy game, solved a complex problem, or remembered every detail of a story? Celebrate these wins.

Challenging Self-Imposed Stigmas

Let's face it, society loves to glorify the visual, but buying into the stigma that you're at a disadvantage? That's not on the agenda. Think of it this way: if someone said you couldn't enjoy a meal because you don't know how to cook it, you'd find that pretty ridiculous, right? The same goes for enjoying life with aphantasia.

- When you catch yourself thinking, "I can't do this because I can't visualize," pause. Ask yourself, "How else can I approach this?" There's always more than one way to skin a cat, metaphorically speaking.

- Surround yourself with positivity. Follow blogs, social media accounts, and podcasts that focus on neurodiversity and personal growth. Their success stories and tips can be powerful antidotes to stigma.

- Create a "brag sheet." List all the abilities and perspectives your aphantasia has given you. Keep it handy for moments of doubt.

- Start a conversation. Whether it's through social media, a blog, or over coffee, talk about your experiences. Highlighting the positives not only boosts your confidence but can also enlighten others.

In wrapping up, remember: your brain might not paint with visuals, but it has a palette all its own, full of sounds, sensations, and words. Embracing your aphantasia isn't just about making peace with your inner world; it's about celebrating it, exploring its nooks and crannies, and sharing its riches with others. Your mental landscape might be unique, but it's undeniably vast, vibrant, and utterly yours.

8.2 Empowering Others: How to Support Someone with Aphantasia

When you're close to someone with aphantasia who is struggling to cope with it, it becomes not just about understanding but also about figuring out the best ways to offer your support and I don't mean walking on eggshells; it's about acknowledging their unique way of experiencing the world, ensuring they feel seen, heard, and included.

Advocating for inclusion means ensuring that aphants have the same opportunities and accommodations as everyone else. Here's where you can make a difference:

* In educational settings, work with teachers and administrators to implement teaching strategies that don't rely solely on visual imagery. This might mean more oral and written instructions or using physical objects for teaching concepts.

* In the workplace, champion for diversity in thought and problem-solving approaches. Encourage teams to recognize the value of different perspectives, including those of individuals with aphantasia.

* Support businesses and content creators who try to be inclusive in their services and products. Whether it's a book that focuses on narrative without prompting readers to visualize or apps designed for non-visual thinkers, showing your support can drive more inclusive innovations.

Supporting someone with aphantasia isn't about focusing on what's missing; it's about acknowledging their experiential difference. Whether through effective communication, providing the right resources, advocating for inclusion, or building a supportive community, your efforts can make a world of difference in recognizing and celebrating the unique ways we all perceive and interact with the world around us.

8.3 The Role of Therapy: Seeking Professional Guidance

Realizing you are wired differently can feel alienating. Sometimes, navigating such an alien world requires a guide, someone who knows the pathways and can help you appreciate the beauty of such wiring. Professional therapy, in many ways, can be that guide, offering not just a helping hand but also a new lens through which to view life.

Therapeutic Approaches

Several therapeutic approaches stand out for their effectiveness in working with individuals who have aphantasia, and some do not. For instance, the stereotypical therapy session with the patient lying on a sofa and being asked to regress to their childhood and picture their earliest memory or being guided by hypnosis to meet up with their younger self and have a chat. These exercises can feel a little pointless to an aphant. Cognitive-behavioral therapy (CBT) on the other hand, helps in identifying and restructuring any thoughts that may be contributing to feelings of isolation or frustration linked to neurodiversity.

Acceptance and Commitment Therapy (ACT) speaks volumes, urging you to accept your distinct cognitive style while dedicating yourself to actions that align with your values and enrich your life. It's all about progress, not in spite of aphantasia, but by integrating it into a deeper comprehension of yourself.

Finding the Right Therapist

Finding a therapist who truly gets it might take a while, yet it's a crucial step. A therapist versed in neurodiversity, with an understanding or specialty in aphantasia, can offer insights and strategies that resonate more deeply with your experiences.

- Start by researching therapists who list neurodiversity as one of their areas of focus. Many therapists now offer brief descriptions of their specialties on their websites or online directories.

- Don't shy away from asking questions before scheduling your first appointment. Inquire about their familiarity with aphantasia and how they've worked with clients on the spectrum of visual imagination.

- Consider online therapy platforms, which can widen your search and connect you with therapists beyond your immediate geographical area, increasing the chances of finding someone with the right expertise.

Therapy Goals and Outcomes

People see therapists for all kinds of reasons, but if your reasons are solely for dealing with aphantasia, your goals might include developing more effective coping strategies for situations where visual imagination is typically relied upon, bolstering self-esteem in the face of societal misconceptions, or finding creative outlets that celebrate your particular way of experiencing the world.

Outcomes from therapy can be transformative, offering a deeper sense of self-acceptance and a toolkit of strategies for working through life. Many find that therapy leads to an increased sense of connectedness — both with others and with their own inner experiences.

Keep a therapy journal to track your goals, progress, and insights. This can be a valuable tool for reflection and can help you see the changes that come as a result of your therapy work.

8.4 Leading by Example

If you are keen to become an advocate for neurodiversity, or just feel the need to share your newfound knowledge on aphantasia, then this section is for you.

Taking a stand isn't just about raising your voice; it's about lighting a path for others to follow, turning individual stories into collective action. Below you will find some ideas for how you can make an impact that resonates far beyond personal circles.

Advocacy Initiatives

Creating waves of change starts with small ripples. Whether it's crafting blog posts that shine a light on aphantasia, organizing community events that increase understanding, or developing resources that aid in education, every effort counts. Here's a look at how you can contribute:

- **Social Media Campaigns**: Use your platforms to share insights, debunk myths, and spread awareness. Hashtags can unify conversations, making it easier for those curious about or affected by aphantasia to connect and engage. Short, engaging posts that share facts, dispel myths, or even offer glimpses into the life of someone with aphantasia can spark interest and conversation. Paradoxically, using visual mediums like infographics or short videos can effectively communicate what aphantasia is to those who rely heavily on visual information. Such content can quickly convey complex ideas, making them accessible and shareable.

- **Host Informative Sessions**: Organizing talks in community centers, libraries, or even online platforms can serve as a beacon for those curious about aphantasia. Tailoring these sessions to different audiences — from school children to professionals — can ensure the message resonates broadly.

- **Educational Workshops**: Partner with local schools to offer workshops. These sessions can educate attendees on what aphantasia is, how it affects those who have it, and ways to support friends or family members.

- **Resource Development**: Compile and create accessible resources—guides, infographics, video content—that educators, employers, and caregivers can use to better understand and accommodate mind-blind individuals.

Role Models and Mentoring

For a newly identified aphant, encountering a role model who shares this trait can be profoundly reassuring. It's a reminder that they're not alone and that aphantasia doesn't limit what they can achieve. If you're further along in your understanding and acceptance of aphantasia, consider how you can serve as a beacon for others:

- **Mentoring**: Connect with individuals newly identifying with aphantasia, offering guidance, support, and encouragement. Your journey can provide valuable insights and hope.

- **Visibility**: Share your accomplishments and how you've adapted to or leveraged aphantasia in your career, hobbies, or personal life. This visibility helps normalize aphantasia and inspires others to embrace their unique perspectives.

Engaging with Wider Media

The media, with its broad reach and influential power, plays a crucial role in shaping perceptions. Engaging with journalists, bloggers, and content creators can amplify the conversation around aphantasia, bringing it into mainstream discourse. Here's how:

- **Pitch Stories**: Reaching out to journalists with pitches that highlight personal stories, recent research, or the impact of aphantasia on creativity and life can lead to broader media coverage.

- **Offer Expertise**: For those well-versed in the nuances of aphantasia, offering to serve as a resource for articles, podcasts, or documentaries can ensure that the information shared is accurate and nuanced.

- **Embrace Opportunities**: Responding to calls for interviews and questionnaires, participating in panels, or writing op-eds for publications can position aphantasia within the broader conversation about neurodiversity and cognitive experiences.

Public Speaking and Outreach

While the thought of public speaking might send shivers down your spine, it's a powerful tool for advocacy. Speaking engagements, whether at conferences, community meetings, or in educational settings, allow you to reach wider audiences, conveying the realities of aphantasia and advocating for inclusivity. Here are some tips to get started:

- **Start Small**: Local community groups or schools can be a great place to begin. These smaller settings offer a supportive environment to hone your message and delivery.

- **Prepare**: Tailor your talk to your audience, ensuring your message is accessible and engaging. Use personal stories to illustrate your points, making the abstract concept of aphantasia more relatable.

- **Practice**: If public speaking isn't your forte, practice is key. Rehearse your presentation with friends or family or record yourself to get your delivery flowing naturally.

Influencing Policy and Change

Lasting change often requires shifts in policy, whether in educational settings, workplaces, or broader societal norms. Here's how you can contribute to these shifts should you choose to:

- **Advocacy Letters**: Write to educational boards, employers, and government representatives, advocating for recognition and accommodations for individuals struggling with aphantasia. Personal stories can be powerful in illustrating the need for change.

- **Join Forces**: Collaborate with organizations focused on neurodiversity and cognitive differences. There's strength in numbers, and collective action can amplify your voice, pushing for policies that acknowledge and support the aphantasic community.

- **Stay Informed**: Keep abreast of policy discussions and legislative changes related to neurodiversity and education. This knowledge can guide your advocacy efforts, ensuring they're timely and informed.

Advocacy Groups

Several organizations and groups have taken up the torch, leading the charge in advocating for a deeper understanding and acceptance of aphantasia. Their work ranges from supporting research to providing resources for those looking to navigate life with aphantasia. A few noteworthy mentions include:

- **The Aphantasia Network**: This platform not only brings together individuals with aphantasia but also offers resources, organizes events, and spearheads awareness campaigns.

- **Project Aphantasia**: Focused on research and advocacy, this initiative works to bring aphantasia into the spotlight, collaborating with scientists and educators to deepen our collective understanding.

- **Aphantasia Support Group**: Operating primarily on social media, this group works tirelessly to advocate for the recognition of aphantasia, using its channels to educate, share stories, and connect individuals.

As we wrap up this exploration of advocacy for aphantasia, remember: your efforts, no matter how small they might seem, contribute to a larger movement towards understanding, acceptance, and inclusion. By standing up for what you believe in, sharing your story, and advocating for change, you're not just shaping your narrative but also paving the way for future generations.

8.5 The Future of Aphantasia: Trends and Predictions

The exploration of aphantasia's neurological foundations is just beginning, with many avenues left to explore. Future research will likely delve deeper into the differences in brain structure and function that characterize the condition, aiming to uncover the root causes and how they manifest in those with aphantasia. This section takes a look at what the coming years might hold for aphantasia research.

Research Directions

The quest for knowledge about aphantasia is gaining momentum, with scientists and psychologists poised and keen to delve deeper into its mysteries. It's likely that future research might include:

- **Longitudinal studies** to track changes in brain activity and connectivity over time in individuals with aphantasia, offering insights into whether these features are static or subject to change.

- **Genetic research** to identify potential hereditary factors contributing to aphantasia, which could point to its origins in brain development. With the suggestion that aphantasia could have genetic foundations, researchers are on the cusp of uncovering familial patterns and potential genetic markers.

- **Comparative studies** to examine how people with aphantasia process other types of sensory information and whether these processes differ from those without the condition.

- **Therapeutic approaches** aimed at enhancing visualization abilities, providing a testing ground for theories about how flexible the brain's visual processing abilities can be.

- **Investigating Neuroplasticity**: The brain's ability to adapt and change is a fascinating field. Upcoming studies might focus on whether targeted exercises could influence the development of mental imagery abilities.

- **Examining the Spectrum**: Recognizing that aphantasia exists on a spectrum, future research could aim to map this landscape more precisely. It would involve identifying subcategories within aphantasia and understanding how different senses are affected.

- **Understanding Emotional Processing**: Does aphantasia influence emotions, empathy, and social interactions?

As scientists delve deeper into how our brains visualize, they inch closer to understanding how we all think, remember, and imagine.

Shifting Perceptions

The narrative around aphantasia is on the brink of a significant shift. In the coming years, we might see:

- **Increased Visibility**: With more individuals coming forward and sharing their experiences, aphantasia will become a more visible part of the conversation around neurodiversity, leading to greater representation in media, literature, and public discourse.

- **Broader Acceptance**: As understanding and visibility grow, so too will acceptance. Aphantasia will increasingly be recognized as a unique way of experiencing the world, rather than a deficiency or anomaly.

- **Normalization**: Just as dyslexia and other cognitive variations have entered the common vocabulary, aphantasia will become a recognized and understood facet of human cognitive diversity.

Global Awareness Efforts

The movement toward global recognition and understanding of aphantasia is gathering strength. Efforts in the pipeline include:

- **International Conferences**: Bringing together researchers, educators, and individuals with aphantasia, these gatherings enable dialogue, share discoveries, and build a global community united by a common interest in understanding and supporting this condition.

- **Awareness Campaigns**: Global campaigns, leveraging social media and partnerships with educational institutions, will aim to educate the public about aphantasia, dispelling myths and enabling an inclusive environment for all.

- **Cross-Cultural Studies**: By examining aphantasia across different cultures, researchers can gain insights into how cultural contexts influence the experience and perception of aphantasia. Such studies will enrich our global understanding of this fascinating cognitive trait.

As we stand at the threshold of these exciting developments, the future for aphantasia looks bright. With every research study, technological advance, shift in perception, and awareness effort, we move closer to a world where aphantasia is not just understood but embraced as an integral part of the human experience.

Conclusion

In our short time together, we embarked on a brief exploration of aphantasia, understanding its challenges and complexities. Our journey began with an introductory look at the aphantasia experience, touching on some personal stories and uncovering the diverse ways in which individuals go about their daily lives without mental imagery. Along the way, we challenged perceptions and misconceptions, uncovered the science behind aphantasia, and explored the myriad ways it does and doesn't affect those living with this condition.

Throughout our exploration, we discovered that aphantasia is not merely a deficiency to be overcome but a unique perspective to be celebrated. We learned the importance of self-acceptance and the value of embracing our neurodiversity, recognizing that our differences don't have to be deficiencies but can actually enrich our world.

Key takeaways from our journey have been the fact that most don't see it as a hindrance at all, yet many have highlighted the significance of community support and the power of connection. We've learned that nurturing connections, both within the aphantasia community and beyond, provides a vital source of strength and understanding, even to those who do not feel it has disabled their life in any way. In celebrating the advantages and unique perspectives that accompany aphantasia, we've shattered stereotypes and paved the way for continued inclusivity and acceptance.

Personally, once I had gotten over the shock of understanding that others really do see pictures in their minds, and once the initial fascination wore off, I quickly came to realize that it has made little apparent difference to my life or my ability to function in society – less impact in fact than my left-handedness. I've simply adapted to find other ways to remember things as most aphants do. I've been teased throughout my life as the one who often doesn't "get" the joke, or after having had a joke explained to me, still asks "I still don't get why that's funny?" to be met with the standard reply, "it's a visual joke", or "I guess you had to be there". I always just shrugged my shoulders and moved on, but since learning about aphantasia, these situations now make perfect sense to me and don't make me feel quite so alienated anymore.

As we conclude our journey, let us reaffirm the concept of neurodiversity and champion the idea that our differences are not deficits but strengths. Let us encourage readers to embrace their unique perspective, recognizing the potential for innovation, creativity, and resilience that lies within. And let us issue a call to action for greater awareness and understanding, urging readers to share their stories, educate others, and advocate for increased research, because there are a large number of aphants out there who do find it a hindrance and who struggle on a daily basis.

Your chance to help others...

Before you go, please allow me to explain the importance of leaving a book review. Not only will you show others where they can find the guidance they are looking for, but you will also be elevating the visibility of aphantasia, and helping to reach people who perhaps have never heard the label before and don't know that support and information is out there.

Sadly, we now live in a world of AI-generated reviews and fake ratings, which Amazon works incredibly hard to weed out. One of the ways you can ensure yours is not removed by Amazon is to simply add a photo to your review. A photo of your paperback, your Kindle, or if you're feeling brave... you reading it!

So, once you have taken the photo, simply find the order on your Amazon account and click "write a product review", or scan the QR code to take you straight to the Amazon USA review page for the book. It really would mean the world to me.

Thank you so much for your support, and your help to spread the word!

About the author

Joanne spent her early years growing up on a dairy farm in south-east England where her fascination with nature began.

After a corporate career in software consultancy, which spanned 25 years, several continents, and numerous bouts of stress and exhaustion, Joanne quit the rat race in 2017 to follow her passions for wildlife and photography. Enrolling on a one-year intensive training course, living in a tent in the African wilderness, Joanne re-trained as a professional safari guide, spending hours each day driving and walking the bush learning all about the flora and fauna of the various sub-saharan habitats. Following graduation, she worked as a guide and later became the manager of a luxury bush camp in the Kafue National Park, Zambia, where she still freelances for a few months each year.

She appreciates that not everyone can disappear into the wilderness for 12 months to improve their physical and mental health, but she believes there are simple steps anyone can take to reconnect with nature and improve their general well-being. Her favorite mantra is "The purpose of life is to live a life of purpose", and since the natural world has always helped her in such a profound way, she has become passionate about giving back, not only to nature but to others by sharing her knowledge, methods and tools through writing self-help books and educating her guests on safari.

Joanne discovered aphantasia in her 40s, and cannot remember a time in her life when she was ever able to mentally create images. Despite being mind-blind and left-handed she is hugely creative and sees her own level of aphantasia as a quirky fascination, not a hindrance. She lives in the UK and when she's not writing, she spends her time rewilding a small piece of ancient woodland, making handmade nature-inspired jewelry and taking photographs.

Find her on Facebookor visit her website for more information www.elementalretail.com

Books by the Same Author

Dream Interpretation
for Better Sleep

Find Meaning in the Messages of Your Subconscious Mind to Build Your Own Dream Dictionary

Start listening to what your subconscious is trying to say — delve deep into your true Self by decoding your dreams!

Dreams are a universal phenomenon everybody experiences. But what are they? Why do we dream? What do they mean?

Have you ever wondered why you are having the same dream repeatedly as if it is telling you something, but you can't just get your head around what it means?

Joanne lays out a short but fascinating read on dreaming for a peaceful sleep. She doesn't want you to be drowned in a sea of technical terms and words. Instead, the book is a **beginner-friendly** tool that will allow you to go deeper into your subconscious as you explore your dreams.

Energetic Herbalism for Beginners

Radically Improve the Effectiveness of Healing Herbs by Matching the Energetic Healing Power of Plants with People and Place
Maybe you have tried a wide range of herbal remedies in the past but found that most didn't work as well for you as they did for others. Or maybe you have heard of plant energetics but are not entirely sure what it means or how it works.

This book simplifies the ancient tradition, walking you step-by-step through each aspect, and explains why taking a "this-for-that" approach to herbology often fails.

Discover the "forgotten" transformative powers of this ancient, but well-proven, herbalist tradition.

Revive and Thrive: Regenerative Gardening for a Sustainable Future

Turn your barren backyard into a productive ecosystem using these affordable tips and techniques
The United Nations stated it takes 1,000 years to generate 3 centimeters of topsoil. We have enough soil for 60 years of crop production at this rate!

At the same time, an endless series of world crises is causing havoc on the food supply. Prices are increasing excessively, making it harder to feed your family a nutritious, fresh diet free of harmful chemicals and pesticides. These issues aren't going to resolve themselves!

This book is a simple and to-the-point exploration of regenerative gardening... starting with soil health and building to a full wildlife-friendly eco-system providing year-round food, this book teaches the importance of getting nature to do the hard work for you so that we can create a sustainable and productive garden for years to come.

Amazon Author Page[1]

---

1. https://www.amazon.com/stores/Joanne-Hedger/author/B0C3Z
ZFGGH

References

- Cleveland Clinic. (n.d.). Aphantasia: What It Is, Causes, Symptoms & Treatment. Retrieved from https://my.clevelan dclinic.org/health/symptoms/25222-aphantasia

- Carey, B. (2020, July 15). Living With Aphantasia, the Inability to Make Mental Images. The New York Times. Retrieved from https://www.nytimes.com/2020/07/15/well/mi nd/aphantasia-mental-images.html

- Medical Xpress. (2023, September). New data help to understand the nature of aphantasia. Retrieved from https://medicalxpress.com/news/2023-09-probing-uni maginable-nature-aphantasia.html

- Wells, S. (n.d.). What Is Aphantasia? Signs, Causes, and Meaning. Well+Good. Retrieved from https://www.wellandgood.c om/what-is-aphantasia/

- Bennett, S., & Partos, T. (2021). Real-world implications of aphantasia: episodic recall ... - NCBI. Retrieved from https://www.ncbi.nlm.nih.gov/pmc/articles/PMC10598423/

- Pearson, J. (2021). What is the relationship between Aphantasia

... ScienceDirect. Retrieved from https://www.sciencedirect.com/science/article/pii/S1053810021000131

- Choosing Therapy. (n.d.). Aphantasia: Definition & How to Cope. Retrieved from https://www.choosingtherapy.com/aphantasia/

- University of St. Augustine for Health Sciences. (n.d.). Science-Backed Memory Tips and Recall Techniques. Retrieved from https://www.usa.edu/blog/science-backed-memory-tips/

- Oboloo. (n.d.). Unlocking the Inner World: A Journey into Aphantasia and ... MentorCruise. Retrieved from https://mentorcruise.com/blog/unlocking-the-inner-world-a-journey-into-aphantasia-and-the-power-of-the-mind/

- Berard, M. (2021). The art of Aphantasia: how 'mind blind' artists create without being able to visualise. The Conversation. Retrieved from https://theconversation.com/the-art-of-aphantasia-how-mind-blind-artists-create-without-being-able-to-visualise-162566

- Harley Therapy. (n.d.). What is Aphantasia? And Does it Affect Mental Health? Retrieved from https://www.harleytherapy.co.uk/counselling/what-is-aphantasia.htm

- Holmes, E. A., & Borchardt, A. (2021). The critical role of mental imagery in human emotion. Frontiers in Psychology, 12, 775485. Retrieved from https://www.ncbi.nlm.nih.gov/pmc/articles/PMC7944105/

- Tico & Tina. (n.d.). Understanding Aphantasia, and Exercises that Might Help ... Retrieved from https://www.ticoandtina.com/understanding-aphantasia-and-exercises-that-might-help-you-learn-to-visualize/

- Taylor, A. (n.d.). Assistive Wearable Tech - Phantaglass - ZENK. Retrieved from http://alexistaylorzenk.com/assistive-wearable-tech#:~:text=Phantaglass%20is%20an%20assistive%20wearable,untapped%20world%20of%20visual%20recollections.

- Mindful Wave Studio. (2019, April 16). Guided Meditation for Aphantasia | Non-Visualization Meditation [Video]. YouTube. Retrieved from https://www.youtube.com/watch?v=4AG_RVMBQQ

- Art of Memory. (n.d.). Aphantasia and Memory Training. Retrieved from https://artofmemory.com/blog/aphantasia/#:~:text=Lynne%20Kelly%20also%20mentioned%20that,I%20always%20use%20physical%20palaces.

- Badenoch, B. (2021). What is the Link Between Mental Imagery and Sensory ... Frontiers in Psychology, 12, 790708. Retrieved from https://www.ncbi.nlm.nih.gov/pmc/articles/PMC8438787/

- Aphantasia Network. (n.d.). Aphantasia Guide. Retrieved from https://aphantasia.com/guide/

- Scientific American. (n.d.). Does Not Being Able to Picture

Something in Your Mind ... Retrieved from https://www.scientificamerican.com/podcast/episode/does-not-being-able-to-picture-something-in-your-mind-affect-your-creativity/

- Taylor, A. (n.d.). What is aphantasia? Inability to visualize images. Fortune. Retrieved from https://fortune.com/well/2023/05/23/what-is-aphantasia-people-cant-visualize-images-in-minds-eye-brain/

- Aphantasia Network. (n.d.). Image Free Thinking. Retrieved from https://aphantasia.com/

- Shah, N., & Smith, A. (2021). The prevalence of aphantasia (imagery weakness) in ... - PubMed. Retrieved from https://pubmed.ncbi.nlm.nih.gov/34872033/

- Houser, L. (2020, July). Learning with Aphantasia. Retrieved from https://www.graduateprogram.org/2020/07/learning-with-aphantasia/

- Harvard Business Review. (2017, May). Neurodiversity Is a Competitive Advantage. Retrieved from https://hbr.org/2017/05/neurodiversity-as-a-competitive-advantage

- Moss, H. (n.d.). How We Move Away From the Stigma of Neurodiversity. Retrieved from https://www.linkedin.com/pulse/how-we-move-away-from-stigma-neurodiversity-haley-moss-esq-#:~:text=Spread%20Empathy%20Above%20All%20Else&text=Empathy%20is%20integral%20to%20moving,spread%20throughout%20those%20aro

und%20us

- Olinger, C. (2021). Narrative practices and autism: Part 1. Dulwich   Centre.   Retrieved   from https://dulwichcentre.com.au/wp-content/uploads/2021/06 /Theory-and-engagement-Part-1-by-Courtney-Olinger.pdf

- Discover Walks. (n.d.). 20 Famous People With Aphantasia. Retrieved from https://www.discoverwalks.com/blog/world /20-famous-people-with-aphantasia/

- Oboloo. (n.d.). Unlocking the Power of Aphantasia: How to Improve Your Business Planning. Retrieved from https://oboloo.com/blog/unlocking-the-power-of-aph antasia-how-to-improve-your-business-planning/

- Aphantasia Network. (n.d.). Aphantasia And Creativity. Retrieved from https://aphantasia.com/topic/creativity/

- Carey, B. (2020, July 15). Living With Aphantasia, the Inability to Make Mental Images. The New York Times. Retrieved from https://www.nytimes.com/2020/07/15/well/mi nd/aphantasia-mental-images.html

Made in the USA
Middletown, DE
12 May 2024

54221874R00077